Get out of Debt and Prosper!

To my wife, Alison, light of my life.

Get out of Debt and Prosper!

The 10-Step Plan that Really Works

Peter Cutler

Thorsons
An Imprint of HarperCollins*Publishers*

Thorsons
An Imprint of GraftonBooks
A Division of HarperCollins*Publishers*
77-85 Fulham Palace Road,
Hammersmith, London W6 8JB

Published by Thorsons 1991

10 9 8 7 6 5 4 3 2 1

Whilst every care has been taken to ensure the accuracy of the
contents of this work, no responsibility for loss occasioned to any
person acting or refraining from action as a result of any statement
in it can be accepted by the author or Publisher.

British Library Cataloguing in Publication Data
Cutler, Peter
Get out of debt and prosper
1. Great Britain. Personal finance
I. Title
332.02400941

ISBN 0 7225 2490 0

Typeset by Harper Phototypesetters Limited,
Northampton, England
Printed in Great Britain by
CollinsManufacturing, Glasgow

Contents

PART 1
The bedrock of change

Whatever the mind of man can conceive and believe, it can achieve.

— *Napoleon Hill*

STEP 1

Make a Commitment to Get Out of Debt!

Britain is facing the greatest explosion of mass personal debt it has ever experienced. Each year there are around 20,000 repossessions of homes from people who can't pay their mortgages. Ten times as many are seriously behind on their mortgage payments. Nearly two million people have trouble paying their fuel bills. Almost half a million people default on their credit card payments. More than 10,000 are declared bankrupt.

These are not idle incompetents, but normal people like you or me who gradually find themselves drowning in debt. The scenario is this—you overspend on credit cards, or take on too big a mortgage; and then an interest-rate hike, the loss of a job, a reduction in commissions, or a downturn in business cuts the ground from under your feet.

You are probably eager to know exactly how to get out of debt. This book will tell you how, in a step-by-step, easy to follow manner. You will discover what the root causes of debt are, and how they might be eliminated. You will see exactly how to assess, plan and monitor your spending in ways that will cause you little inconvenience and which will have immediate benefits. You will be able to calculate precisely the cost of credit, and understand how to harness the powerful engine of compound interest for your own benefit, ensuring your future prosperity.

However, before you jump straight into the programme, it is important to understand the background to the debt explosion. You will realize that you are not alone, and that we have all suffered from a degree of financial manipulation by the Government and the organizations which owe their existence and financial well-being to borrowers.

The Debt Explosion

The debt situation has been *engineered* chiefly by financial institutions, so it is no surprise to see that the problem has increased over recent years. In the early 1980s, there was actually a credit famine, particularly for mortgages. An individual was only allowed to borrow up to two and a half times his or her income—as an absolute maximum. Institutional lenders practised prudence. Furthermore, unless you had been with a building society for several years, you were not even considered eligible for a loan. It was then necessary to have a long-term relationship with a building society or a bank when you wanted credit.

The mortgage famine of the time was caused by a shortage of personal savings. With the loosening of financial regulations under the Thatcher Government, many more institutions—especially banks—were allowed to lend money for mortgages, and what was more, banks could lend out more money than they actually held to prospective buyers.

Building societies were at first restricted from doing this, but later they too began to borrow money 'wholesale' and then to relend it. Companies were even set up in this manner specifically to offer mortgages. Consequently, there was an explosion of availability of credit for mortgages, and the great home-buying spree began. As house prices rose and more institutions piled into the market, the amount which people could borrow moved upwards. Soon loans of three times income became commonplace, then three and a half, and then four. Home purchasers were even offered low-start mortgages, with interest payments in the early years being postponed and added to their repayment burden in later years.

Even people who had formerly been considered uncreditworthy began to join the rush to buy. If you did not object to a higher interest rate charge you could buy a house even if your income was uncertain; or if you shared with other buyers.

Another sinister development took place at this time. Suddenly, everybody began to get invitations to take out credit cards. Again, not so long ago credit cards were considered to be the prerogative of a fortunate few high earners. Until the 1980s, much of the plastic which was issued was on a charge card basis. This meant that you could borrow any amount, but you had to repay it in full within a month.

Charge cards are convenient sources of free credit, which also exert financial discipline on their holders. Credit cards are very different. As we all know, you only have to pay 5 per cent of the outstanding balance. What the lenders don't tell you is that if you repay only the minimum amount on a loan of say, £1,000, at current interest rates it will take you more than *eight* years to repay the sum borrowed! Consequently, the number of defaults on credit card debt has risen rapidly, and credit card interest rates have remained extortionate partly to take account of this situation.

Another little-known cost of debt is the price you pay for a mortgage. Even if you borrow the relatively small sum of £30,000 so that you can take full advantage of the mortgage-interest tax-relief concession, you will wind up paying more than three times the amount borrowed. After 25 years of paying off a £30,000 mortgage at an interest rate of 15 per cent per annum you will have paid a total of £90,720 back to the lender. No wonder there has been so much competition for mortgage business!

The credit explosion is part of a long-term economic cycle which has profound implications for all our lives. For the moment, it is enough to say that after the credit boom comes the credit crunch. The almost unimaginable debts which have been accumulated on an international scale are in the process of being liquidated, often by force. This is true for countries as much as for companies and individuals.

The liquidation of international debt is a necessary and constructive process, but for many people it is a painful one. With it comes falling prices of assets, such as houses, which many people once thought could only increase in value. We will leave a fuller explanation of this cycle until the postscript to this book. It will suffice to say here that the quicker you can voluntarily get out of debt, then the quicker you can take advantage of the economic cycle and achieve financial prosperity.

Being in Debt Does Not Have to Be a Permanent Condition!

If you stop to think about it, you have not always been in debt—quite probably your situation changed only gradually. Not so very long ago, you probably considered yourself as 'poor', in terms of income, but at the same time you had little or no debt. As you were not considered creditworthy you had not been offered all those credit cards, mortgages and bank loans. Now, however, you may have a much higher income than that of a few years ago, with an incomparably higher debt load.

There is no law of nature that says you have to take on all this trouble as your monetary standard of living rises. Whether your income has recently fallen after a long period of increases, or whether you are still on a rising income with a rising debt load, you should recognize that debt does not have to be a permanent condition. You decided to get into debt, so you can decide to get out of debt! It really is that simple.

The Debt Habit

Getting into debt is a habit, just like any other. Debtors tend to start young by borrowing a few pounds off a friend or a relative. Then the amounts get bigger and the repayment times lengthier. When they land their first job they probably also get their first credit card, and are suddenly able to buy all the things they really want without having to do all that boring business of working hard and saving.

Many people in their early twenties take on a large mortgage as soon as they possibly can, at the maximum possible level, because that is what everybody else seems to do, and, as we saw in the late 1980s, property prices were rising so fast that young people were told they would be mad not to get onto the property ladder. That's what everybody said, anyway, *especially* employees of the banks, building societies and estate agents.

Unfortunately, with some people the debt habit goes even further and becomes a compulsion. These are the people who go on spending binges in order to 'cheer themselves up', equating the brief thrill of possessing new material goods or elaborate services (such as meals out, a new hair-style or foreign holidays) with happiness. In such sad cases the compulsion often hides a deep unhappiness. The thrill doesn't last long, and the compulsion remains.

There is another category: those who are very poor and borrow for necessities, as well as for emergencies. (All debtors borrow for emergencies, because they never have contingency funds available.)

It is not easy for people on very low incomes to see how they are supposed to get out of debt—they believe that they are caught in the vicious cycle of a poverty trap. How are you supposed to get out of a poverty trap if the State won't give you any more money, or if the hard-hearted boss pays you starvation wages?

For people in this position, it may seem incredible that affluent middle class people on high incomes could also be deeply in debt.

Yet debt knows no class distinctions. Even company directors on £100,000 a year can be mortgaged up to the hilt and deeply in hock to the banks. They might be just as worried as the poor, and just as indebted in terms of multiples of income.

There is even the phenomenon of 'distress debting'. As interest rates rise, otherwise apparently affluent people borrow to maintain their standard of living. Of course, in this desperate attempt to keep up with the Jones's, they are all the more likely to end up poor. This used to be one of my favourite tricks—borrowing to keep up with my increasingly affluent friends while I was struggling along on a low income.

We will go more deeply into why all these people from varied backgrounds and with huge income differentials find themselves in the same boat. For the moment, we might like to note a few of the signals likely to indicate that you are going into the danger zone.

Alarm Signals

If we stop to think about how much future income we are sacrificing in order to indulge our transient whims for playthings, fancy clothes and meals out, then we would be absolutely horrified at the price we pay in terms of interest on the debt and time spent earning the income to service it.

What happens is that the debt treadmill is not measured by the debtor in terms of real money: you don't think about how much you are actually paying for the things you buy. Instead, you measure debt in terms of your existing commitments—how much you can afford to pay monthly—or in terms of your credit ceiling—how much you are permitted to borrow.

Your credit card statements even tell you how much you are able to 'spend' each month! Oh good, you think, I can 'spend' £300 this month. If the gap between what you already owe and the credit ceiling is too narrow, the chances are that you can ask for extra credit over the phone—or get another credit card or bank loan. After all, your wages are bound to rise next year to meet the extra commitments, aren't they? So the tortured thinking goes.

When you are really getting in over your head, there are a number of tricks to help you to avoid reality. All of these are alarm signals. My favourite trick was to toss newly-arrived credit card statements into a drawer, without bothering to open them. I figured that I could go two or three months without annoying the credit card company too much, although they would print a rude message about my overdue repayment on the bill, so that when I did get round to paying it the bank clerk would see it. Embarrassing as this might be, I could live with it.

Hand in hand with an ability to throw credit card statements into an obscure corner goes the chronic debtor's refusal to quantify the extent of his or her debt. Not only do you have a deliberately hazy notion of the exact amount, but you refuse to keep an accurate balance of your bank account.

When I finally sat down to tot up the full extent of my debt, I was horrified to find that it was well over £40,000. In carrying out the exercise, I had to rack my brain to discover exactly what I owed to whom. It was easy to forget casual debts to friends, or money I 'owed' myself—such as money paid out from a pension fund which I had promised to save, but had instead spent on immediate consumption. What I had vaguely considered a manageable £10,000 debt quickly quadrupled in size.

Another aspect of the refusal to quantify debt is the debtor's unwillingness to read the small print on credit agreements or balance statements. When you are heavily in the red, it is easier not to notice or not to think about the precise rate of interest you are paying. When you finally do pay off a credit card instalment, you do so at the minimum rate, without paying any attention to the amount of interest and capital you have repaid. On the other hand, when you have money in the bank, your attitude is reversed, and you fret about paying the tiniest amount of interest.

How Bad Is Your Debt Problem?

So far, we have looked at the ways in which debt can become a habit. It is now time for you to take stock of your situation, and to discover exactly what kind of debtor you are. There are basically three categories, which I have called *marginal, dangerous* and *chronic*. While the three categories correspond to different degrees of indebtedness, all can be cured through positive action.

It is worth taking the time to discover exactly what your situation is by doing this simple quiz. Score each answer as indicated, and add up the results to discover which category you fall into. Please remember— you must be honest with yourself. This is not the time for self-delusion, you are embarking on a course which will change your life!

Quiz

1. When a credit card statement arrives, do you:
   - a   open it immediately and pay it on time (1 point)
   - b. open it at a later date and pay it on time (2 points)
   - c. forget about it until you know that it is overdue (3 points)
   - d. pay instalments only when you are threatened with court action (5 points)?

2. Do you know what the current interest rate is on your mortgage?
   - a. yes, exactly (1 point)
   - b. guess correctly within 0.5 per cent of the true figure (2 points)
   - c. no exact idea (3 points).

3. Do you know what interest rate you are paying monthly on your credit cards?
   - a. yes, exactly (1 point)
   - b. correct within 0.25 per cent (2 points)
   - c. no idea (3 points).

4. What multiple of income is your outstanding mortgage at?
   - a. less than two (1 point)
   - b. 2 to 3 times (2 points)
   - c. more than three (3 points).

5. Is your home, at current market value, worth more or less than you paid for it?
   - a. more (1 point)
   - b. about the same (3 points)
   - c. less (5 points).

6. If you rent your home, is your share of the rent:
   - a. less than 20 per cent of your income (1 point)
   - b. 20 to 35 per cent of your income (3 points)
   - c. more than 35 per cent of your income (5 points)?

7. Do you know, without looking it up, what your outstanding debts total?
   - a. yes, exactly (1 point)
   - b. guessed within £500 of the true figure (2 points)
   - c. no real idea (3 points).

8. How many credit cards do you own?
   a. 1 (1 point)
   b. 2 to 3 (3 points)
   c. 4 or more (5 points).

9. Do you regularly use store cards, without immediately paying off the balance?
   a. yes, at least monthly (3 points)
   b. sometimes (2 points)
   c. never use them (0 points).

10. If you have an outstanding balance on one or more store cards is it:
   a.   more than £1,000 (5 points)
   b. £500 to £1000 (3 points)
   c. under £500 (2 points)?

11. Have you taken out any new line of credit during the last year (mortgage, bank loan, credit card, hire purchase)?
   a. yes (3 points)
   b. from more than one source (5 points)
   c. no (0 points)

12. Add up all your debts, including your outstanding mortgage. Is the total:
   a. more than twice your income (1 point)
   b. more than three times your income (3 points)
   c. more than four times your income (5 points).

13. Does your bank current account pay interest when in credit?
   a. yes (0 points)
   b. no (3 points).

14. Do you save money (pension schemes not included)?
   a. yes, regularly (0 points)
   b. sometimes (3 points)
   c. never (5 points).

15. If you had a windfall of £5,000, would you:
    a. use it to pay off your debts (3 points)
    b. use most for debt repayment and spend the rest (5 points)
    c. save all of it because you have no debts (0 points)
    d. stay in debt and spend the lot (7 points).

Quiz Results

Add up the points for each question you have answered.

10 to 15 points: you really do seem to have your finances well under control. No need to worry about debt—just turn to the section on saving and investment to enhance your wealth!

15 to 25 points: you are drifting into the marginal category of debtors. You need to tighten control of your finances and pay more attention to where the money goes.

25 to 35 points: be careful—you are drifting into the danger zone! Either your income must rise or your expenditure fall to avoid the perils of a sudden shock to your finances. Beware of going into a debt tunnel without knowing the way out.

More than 35 points: you are firmly in the danger zone, but don't panic. By completing this quiz you are facing up to your situation, and that is the first step on the road to recovery. Remember, your debt situation does not have to be permanent.

Understanding Yourself

If you have taken the trouble to do this quiz, then you have been brave and honest with yourself, and you have taken a first step towards financial recovery. It is a sad fact that the root of a person's debt problem is not necessarily lack of money. Chronic debtors, if they are truthful with themselves, may well have blown the windfall offered in question 15. People who do not get into debt will survive even on low incomes, barring absolute poverty and catastrophe. Equally, people with a debt mentality will tend to get into debt even on incomes much higher than the national average (£12,000 p.a.)

It may be difficult for you to understand and accept, but a tendency to get deeply in debt is almost certainly rooted in a negative view of yourself. A person with a poor self-image will feel inadequate, and is likely to carry out damaging actions against him- or herself. Often this damaging behaviour is subconscious: it is carried out at a level below the normal level of conscious understanding. The debtor will always invent plausible excuses to account for his or her behaviour. Yet that behaviour may reveal deeply held self-destructive motives.

Many people establish a deep seated belief in their own inadequacy at an early age. Perhaps you were continually rejected by a parent when you tried to help out with small tasks. Maybe you were told you were clumsy, useless and no-good for so long that you began to believe it. Or you simply did not get all the affection you felt you needed from your parents. These feelings of rejection and hurt remain. They may be buried deeply and may not be apparent to your conscious mind, but they will emerge later in adult life. In some cases a lack of self-regard may manifest itself in a pathetic attempt to 'keep up with the Jones's'. The richer your friends get, the more likely they are to buy expensive cars, go out to restaurants, etc. In order to save face, you may try to do the same thing.

For some people, overspending may be a reaction to deep unhappiness. For example, a woman who finds it difficult to form relationships might blow £100 or more on a new outfit, to cheer herself up. The clothes pile up in her wardrobe, often worn only once, and are then tossed carelessly aside. Her feelings of inadequacy and unhappiness do not dissipate, but the number of her creditors grows.

Sometimes people borrow heavily to start up a new business, often securing the debt on their home. However, a lack of business acumen, under-financing or a host of other factors may cause the business to fail, as it does in most cases. Sometimes, at a deeply subconscious level, the would-be businessperson might even *plan* to fail in business. Some people will borrow from every possible source, including banks, friends, relatives and loan sharks in order to give the appearance that their business is still functioning, and thus to maintain a façade of success. Such would-be entrepreneurs may end up so heavily in debt that they may even attempt suicide. Debt can seem like an unbearable load on your shoulders, but believe me, by changing your attitude it *is* possible to eliminate debt from your life.

It is all too easy to blame debt on external circumstances. Do not allow yourself this alibi. Debt is caused by our own decisions and actions, which are informed not merely by our conscious mind—the thoughts we can hear in our heads, chugging away all day, but also by our subconscious mind, existing just below the surface of our awareness. If, subconsciously, we believe that we do not deserve to be successful, then we are likely to fail, get into debt and generally keep ourselves at whatever level of life our innermost thoughts have decided should be our lot. You will learn more about the vital role of subconscious programming in the next chapter.

You may think you have only been a little careless, having gone out and overspent on your first credit card. But, if you are reading this book, the chances are the problem has gone a lot deeper than that, for a lot longer. And even if overspending is your first offence, then you would be wise to nip it in the bud now, by examining your motives.

I cannot play the role of psychologist, and go into all your motives for running up debts. However, I am going to insist that you recognize that you have a problem, and that you get some support from relatives, friends, or even professionals to help you analyze and deal with it. (See the list of helpful organizations in Appendix 1) What is more, you can help yourself enormously, gaining new courage, confidence and a 'can-do' attitude by following the programme I am about to outline.

You Are Responsible

The first and sometimes the most difficult principle to accept is that you are entirely responsible for your actions. Nevertheless, it is always much easier to blame someone or something else for your poverty and debt problems: a favourite being society itself, or the 'system', which many people believe is stacked against them. You can blame your problems on poor education, general bad luck, or hundreds of other factors. People are always ready to tell us that the sources of our problems are external. Politicians make a living out of telling us this, as do some educators and influential journalists. It is so easy to blame 'the Government', 'foreign competition', 'interest rates', or any other variable one cares to think of. Obviously such elements may play their part, but we must accept responsibility for being influenced by these external factors. We can decide whether or not to go into debt; how we wish to live; and in what ways we wish to better ourselves.

If you can accept that your way of life and your debt situation are of your own making, then you have taken the first positive step towards dealing with it. And what you have made you can also unmake.

You *Can* Get Out of Debt!

It is important to realize that your debt situation is only temporary, however bad it may appear to you right now. Once you have decided to get out of debt, you are already on the road to reducing, and eventually eliminating your debt.

The second point to consider is that whatever happens you are not going to starve, and that you will continue to have a roof over your head, even if you are presently having difficulty paying the mortgage. Most important of all, there is no need to panic because here and now you are all right. Take some time to take stock and remind yourself of all the good things you enjoy in life, and that you will continue to enjoy—family, friends, relationships, and surroundings.

Try to understand, too, that you have both a moral and personal duty to work your way out of debt. After all, people have provided you with the goods and services that you have enjoyed, and you should return to them payment for their labour. This is not to say that the finance companies do not bear some responsibility for putting perhaps too much temptation your way. Nevertheless, you chose to borrow the money and you have a duty to repay it.

What you are not going to do is declare bankruptcy. That option is not fair to your creditors, or yourself. Declare yourself bankrupt and you will lose everything and have to start again from scratch. Eliminate debt from your life in a progressive and sensible fashion and you will retain your possessions and your self-respect.

Lastly, you are not, absolutely not, going to attempt to borrow more money in order to get out of debt. This includes borrowing secured loans at apparently attractive interest rates, advertised as enabling you to clear all your credit card bills and bank loans in one fell swoop. Instead, you are going to plan and work your way out of debt.

When you have got out of debt through your own efforts, you will have achieved at least three invaluable benefits. You will have proved to yourself just how strong and capable you are—having gone from an apparently 'impossible' situation to one of harmony and plenty. Your relationships with your family and friends will have improved immeasurably, and you will be enjoying even stronger bonds of affection and friendship with those people who are close to you. And you will have placed yourself in a position to develop your self-fulfilment even further, however you define it—but almost certainly involving health, wealth and happiness.

There are a number of simple tools which will send you on your way out of debt and into happiness and prosperity. They are not difficult, you won't need years of rigorous training, exceptional mental or physical ability, or any other attributes, save one. *You must be committed to resolving your problems.* This commitment involves following the programme outlined in this book. It doesn't take much time, but it does take commitment.

You must decide, resolve, and believe that you are going to get out of debt.

Points to Remember

- Recognize that you have a debt problem, as do thousands of other people. You are not alone!

- Understand that your debt situation is only temporary, and that it is within your power to resolve it.

- Enjoy the here and now—you are not starving or sleeping on the street.

- Accept that bankruptcy or further borrowing is not an option. You have a duty to repay your debt.

- Enlist the support of your family or very close friends—get the problem out into the open so you can gain some perspective on the reasons why you are in debt.

- Realize that in dealing with debt you will put yourself on the road to wealth and happiness in your personal life.

- Make a commitment to solve your debt problem.

STEP 2

Develop a positive mental attitude

The first chapter of this book concentrated on the negative aspect of getting into debt, explaining how debt is closely bound up with lack of confidence and a negative view of the world. However, the other side of the coin is the fact that an improved self-image really *can* lead to prosperity.

The source of prosperity, like the source of debt, is internal, not external. It lies with you. The way you think affects the way you act, and the results of those actions. So let us first consider *how* thinking occurs.

The Conscious, Unconscious and Subconscious Minds

The *conscious* mind is the one we all know and of which we are aware. All those thoughts that whirl through your head all day are products of the conscious mind. Much of what we think is repetitive, such as thoughts about what we look like, how much money we owe, or how overweight we are.

When we have problems, we usually look to the conscious mind to solve them. On a superficial level, our intellect—the conscious mind at work—may appear to do the trick, finding solutions to our problems. Yet many of these 'solutions' prove to be only temporary, or the problems appear to be intractable, so we may remain unhappy and unfulfilled.

The *unconscious* mind is a massive storehouse of all our thoughts and memories. Everything we have ever thought or done goes in there, and is kept on file. Most of the time we are unaware that this is happening, but nonetheless it goes on constantly. Only under extreme stress is the unconscious mind likely to yield up its treasures.

An acquaintance of mine was once held up by terrorists in Africa and very nearly killed. He told me that as he thought he was about to be shot dead his life flashed before him at blinding speed in a series of vivid memories. These memories lodged in his unconscious finally revealed themselves.

The *subconscious* mind is a third level of brain power which can be used to achieve dramatic results. The subconscious mind is similar to the unconscious mind, in that it absorbs information unbeknownst to the conscious mind. However, the subconscious is able to synthesize the vast storehouse of information in the unconscious to inform our actions.

Unfortunately, the vast majority of people go through life unaware of the power and potential of their subconscious mind, which may not appear to be accessible. It is the conscious mind of which we are normally aware. Only in exceptional circumstances do avenues open up into the subconscious. These give rise to those infallible hunches which we often call our 'slxth sense', and which we ignore at our peril.

The subconscious mind acts like a huge computer, synthesizing and analyzing all of the data available to the other two 'minds'—the conscious and unconscious. It is also immensely important to our perceptions of ourselves. The subconscious is constantly working away, feeding in data to shape our conscious thoughts. Our self-inflicted inadequacies are the result of negative thoughts whlch we have fed into our subconscious mind.

Just as negative thoughts create negative outcomes; positive thoughts bring about positive outcomes. When we imagine ourselves in a prosperous state, the subconscious is busy absorbing the data and storing it. Positive images replace our previous negative ones, and begin to affect our lives through our conscious actions. This is quite remarkable.

You Are What You Think

The subconscious mind works with what it is fed. If you feed it positive thoughts, then you may expect positive results. Feed it negative thoughts and the reverse happens. You will remember that we located the debtor's problem as based fundamentally on an inadequate self-image. To achieve prosperity, this inadequate image must be replaced with a positive one.

Think of your brain as a kind of amplifier. Whatever thoughts you have at the conscious level tend to be repeated thousands of times.

These thousands of repetitions are pumped into your subconscious mind, (the major part of your brain), and then out into the universe. Thoughts are a powerful form of energy. If your conscious mind is constantly repeating the same negative thoughts, then they will feed through to the subconscious mind and become part of your character. If you keep telling yourself that you are stupid and will always be in debt, then your inner self, dominated by the subconscious mind, will begin to believe it.

The only way to combat this negative self-image is to repeat equally often that you will be successful, and that you will rid yourself of your debt burden. Replace negative thoughts with positive ones.

So this is one of the first ways to reprogramme yourself for success. Be kind to yourself. Turn the negative into the positive. For example, instead of saying: 'It's hopeless, I'll never get out of debt, my expenses are too high and my income is too low.' You will replace this negative statement even as it starts with: 'It's hope . . . What am I saying? Of *course* I will get out of debt, I am enthusiastic and persistent.'

You are Unique

Just in case you are feeling really down in the mouth, and are finding it hard to adopt a positive attitude, you must remember a fact of vital importance, which no person or situation can ever take away from you. You are unique!

No one person on this earth is exactly like another. We all look different, and we all have different talents and combinations of talents. Just think about that for a moment. Everybody is good at something, whether it is sport or handicrafts, writing, music, caring for others, or a thousand other ways of expressing your humanity. Every person on this earth has at least one talent, and if you take the time to discover them, you will find you have many. If you are not sure about what your talent is, then think about what you like doing. The chances are you will be good at it; and if you are good at it, then someone, or lots of people, might *pay* you to be good at it.

So, next time you find yourself thinking negative thoughts, be kind to yourself and remember that you are special as are your talents. Techniques for helping you make the most of your talents will be discussed later in this chapter.

Thoughts Become Things

There is another aspect of thinking which is often overlooked. Thoughts are a form of energy. Basic physics tells us that energy cannot be destroyed—it is always converted into another form. Material things such as food, houses, cars and luxuries are also forms of stored energy.

When you desire a thing, you can see it in your mind's eye—you *visualize* it. If you are hungry you visualize the food you would like to eat, and you know how good it will taste before eating it. If you are thinking of buying a car, you take great care to find out all you can about the make and model you will purchase, you will have a clear picture in your mind of what you want from having examined similar models and from reading the sales literature.

If you venture into areas where there is as yet nothing concrete, such as getting a new job, or starting a business from scratch, you usually have an image in your mind of what you are looking for. The clearer the picture, the more likely it is that the job or business opportunity will take shape in reality. You are converting the energy of your thoughts into solid shape!

Successful people always visualize exactly what they require before embarking on a course of action. They construct a mental picture in great detail. They will often eventually say that what results from their actions is 'just like they pictured it'. Napoleon Hill, in his famous book *Think and Grow Rich* (Wilshire Book Co.,1970) puts it very bluntly and succinctly. He says, 'Thoughts are things'.

How to Develop a Positive Mental Attitude

It is clear that every action you take starts with the impulse of thought. So you must think positive thoughts. When you embark on a programme to eradicate debt from your life, you have to overcome quite a history of negative thinking. The accumulation of bad thoughts about yourself and your abilities is there, but it is all in the past—you can, and will decide to change your future.

You can develop a positive mental attitude through the techniques outlined below. Most of all, you must tell yourself regularly that you are capable of improving your life and that you will find a way to overcome your difficulties. The more you tell yourself this, the quicker it will happen. Why not do it a thousand times a day? This will still be only a small part of the thoughts which flash through your conscious mind every day.

Of course, the very act of taking charge of your life and beginning a programme to eliminate debt will do an enormous amount to enhance your self-image. However, it is possible to speed up the process and accelerate your drive to eliminate debt and establish prosperity. This can be done through the powerful psychological tool of visualization.

Imagine a Better Life

As we have said, your mind reproduces the images it is fed. If you imagine yourself poor and hopeless, then that is how you will be. Conversely, if you imagine yourself debt-free, happy and prosperous, that too will be the result.

Can you dare to hope for a better life? Can you, for example, visualize your ideal home? If you visualize it frequently, and in detail, you will be pumping in images of a goal which your busy subconscious mind will help you to reach. It will compute your talents and assets, whatever they are, and come up with an infallible plan for realizing this goal. The more precise and detailed you are about your requirements, the more likely you are to achieve them.

If you are in debt and under stress, the chances are that your personal life is suffering. The daily visualization of more harmony with your family and friends will lodge deep within your subconscious, and prompt you to behave in a manner that will make improved relationships a reality.

One of the best ways to use visualization is to list all the attributes you feel you need to get out of debt and prosper. You will need to implant these deep within your subconscious mind by repeatedly vocalizing and visualizing them. It is best to do this first thing in the morning and last thing at night. These subconscious promptings, also called 'affirmations', will help to charge you up for the day's efforts early in the morning; and help to instil these characteristics deep in your subconscious mind late at night. Your personality and ability to achieve tasks will inevitably begin to improve in tandem with your efforts.

Your chosen list of characteristics and situations is your own affair. But do state your objectives clearly, visualizing them as you do so. The clearer your mind's eye view, the closer you are to success.

Some Examples of Characteristics

Although the characteristics you wish to acquire, and the goals you wish to achieve are very much personal ones, by way of an example I shall list some common characteristics which students of success may wish to attain. Many of them feature on my own list.

- I am relaxed and confident, and go my own way in life.
- I am enthusiastic about my aims and achievements.
- I do not procrastinate—I do it now!
- I am full of energy, and the more I do the more energetic I get.
- I awake feeling refreshed and optimistic.
- I do not worry—I take action to deal with worries.
- I achieve and exceed my goals.
- I enjoy good health.
- I have an excellent memory, which is improving all the time.
- My relationships with others both at work and socially are excellent.
- I motivate people to work willingly and well.
- I enjoy meeting new people.
- I enjoy learning new skills.
- I work with absolute concentration.
- I work very efficiently.
- I am decisive, and accurate in my judgement.

When you list desirable characteristics in this manner, you must state them as if you are already in possession of those traits which you wish to achieve. Your subconscious mind will absorb the information you are feeding it, and will dictate your behaviour accordingly. You may wish to outline your characteristics in much more detail than I have done here.

You will find that apart from visualizing first thing in the morning and last thing at night, the technique is very helpful when you face a stressful situation. For example, if you are going to a job interview, you should 'see' yourself there, relaxed and confident, and impressing the interviewers. If you are trying to repay a particularly troublesome debt, you will find it helpful to imagine yourself writing the cheque, or receiving a statement showing that the balance is cleared. If you are facing a difficult examination, visualize yourself receiving the certificate with the required grade on it. Work hard on your subconscious image of yourself, and you will pass with flying colours.

You may have heard of these methods of affirming positive thoughts before now, and you may have dismissed them as silly and childish. How can you sit there talking to yourself out loud without feeling foolish? The fact is that you can, and you must! The spoken word is powerful, and the written word more powerful still. There is usually somewhere you can sit quietly in your home, even if you have to lock yourself in the bathroom or spare bedroom. Don't worry about what your family, friends or neighbours might think. Enlist the help of your partner or family—point out to them that your debt situation is serious, and that you are taking serious steps to resolve it.

Exercise your Body as well as your Mind

As well as beginning a programme of affirmations and visualizations to bring about a change in your mental attitude, it is important to introduce a physical exercise programme. The main reason for this is that there is an established link between physical fitness and positive thinking. When you exercise, a family of chemicals named *endorphins* are released into your bloodstream which act like opiates, giving you a natural high, and causing you to feel optimistic. This explains in part why some people become obsessive about exercise. I am not suggesting that you set out to become an Olympic athlete, but a half-hour exercise programme at least three times a week, plus at least one session a week of your favourite sport, is going to do you the power of good. It is worth achieving, as the Romans said, *Mens sana in corpore sanum*: a sound mind in a healthy body. Regular exercise will give you much more enthusiasm for tackling your debt problems, and will help give you the mental and physical stamina you need to ensure success.

Know what You Want

If you want to improve your life, then you must define what exactly it is that you want! It is extraordinary how few people can tell you exactly what they want out of life. Try asking your friends and neighbours! Do they know, for example, how much money they want to earn next year? Do they have any real idea of the kind of house and neighbourhood in which they wish to live? Or do they just have a vague idea of an income or a house, not very far removed from what they have now?

The natural law is: you get what you expect to get, or the person who aims high gets more. To put the principle yet another way: we are where we want to be. If you want to be in another situation, then you had better define exactly where and what it is.

Fewer than one person in a hundred really knows what they want out of life. They haven't defined it, they can't tell you in detail if asked, and the chances are that they never will. One of the advantages of being heavily in debt is that it forces you to confront your shortcomings and to re-assess your life. The experience of planning and working your way out of debt, if properly handled in line with the principles outlined in this book, will make you stronger and more prosperous.

However, to really reach the heights you had better decide *now* exactly where you want to be.

Another vital aspect of goal-setting is that you must also define *when* you want to achieve your goals. You must be very precise about it. For example, you might state definitely that 'I will have paid off all of my credit card debt by 31 December next year'. You will in fact probably have both short-term and long-term goals, which you would be wise to state and give time limits for. Again, you must decide which goals are most important to you, and establish deadlines that are realistic.

The reason you must set a time limit is that it helps your subconscious mind work more rigorously. Deadlines focus your efforts. You have to know not just *where* you are going but *when* you expect to get there! You wouldn't arrange to meet someone without this vital information, would you? So why go through life without a map and a timetable? You must tell life what you want of it. One of my favourite ditties sums up the principle very nicely:

> I bargained with Life for a penny
> And Life would pay no more
> However I begged at evening,
> When I counted my scanty store.
> For Life is a just employer
> He gives you what you ask
> But once you have set the wages
> Why, you must bear the task.
> I worked for a menial's hire
> Only to learn, dismayed,
> That any wage I had asked of Life
> Life would have willingly paid

From *Think and Grow Rich,* by Napoleon Hill

A third feature of goal-setting is that you must write down your objectives, even if you know them by heart. This follows the same principle as writing down your affirmations, and repeating them out loud.

The written word has power, and the act of writing further etches your goals indelibly into your subconscious mind. You should refer to your goals frequently, reading them aloud and visualizing your achievements. I have written down my goals and the characteristics I will need to achieve them in my leather-bound desk diary, where they are easily accessible. You may like to do the same, or put them in a notebook close to your bedside. Be sure to write them in a quality notebook with a fine pen, for they are goals of quality.

Examples of Goals

You may be highly ambitious or only modestly so. However, you must define *exactly* what you want. Start with the small, simple goals, and work up to the bigger ones. For example:

- By 30 June this year I will have paid off my credit card bill in full.
- By the end of this month I will have started a new training course to improve my job prospects.
- By the end of next month I will have taken a long weekend break with my family in Cornwall.
- Next year, on my birthday, I will pay in cash for a family car.
- By three years from today, I will have cleared all of my outstanding debts.

These are merely examples—you must decide exactly what it is you want, and the time limits necessary to achieve your goals.

One word of caution is relevant here. At the moment, you are probably suffering from a poor self-image, especially if you are heavily in debt and at your wit's end with worry. The thought of achieving ambitious goals may appear inconceivable to you. This is why it is often a good idea to start with smaller, easily achievable goals, and work your way up to the more ambitious ones.

While you must define your long-term goals, you will also find it vital to define weekly and monthly ones. For example, you should get the week off to a good start by writing down those things which you must accomplish by the end of the week. This discipline takes about five minutes, but pays dividends by keeping you on course towards your larger goals. Otherwise, there is always a temptation to keep putting off the time when you will sit down and tackle your debts, or look for ways of boosting your income.

It is also vital to realize that goals will be meaningless unless you are passionate about them. It is emotion as well as thought that produces results. This is the key to success. If you want something badly, then you will find a way, with the aid of your subconscious mind, to get it.

It is worth remembering that goals can change. You may decide that the effort of getting something is not worth the necessary sacrifice. Or you may find as you grow more prosperous that things you thought you wanted are not so important, after all. I used to want to drive a luxury car, to make up for the old banger I was forced to drive during my debt-ridden days. I now drive a comfortable saloon car with which I am very happy, so my luxury car goal has receded.

You may find that you achieve some of your goals remarkably quickly. You then have a choice—either set new ones or concentrate more on the big goals left on your list. It is your choice —you can make and re-make your fate.

As someone who has suffered from an inadequate self-image for years, I have found that it has not been quite enough only to imagine and visualize my goals. I find it is very convincing to the subconscious mind to keep telling myself that I *deserve* to be successful. Constant affirmation of the fact that you deserve something is a concrete and quick way to get it.

Once you have started to practise using your powerful subconscious computer, reprogramming it with instructions that will enable you to achieve specific goals, then things will start to happen to make those goals come true. You may be a sceptic and put it down to coincidence, or you may be more credulous and think of it as miraculous. It is neither—the principles outlined here are not new, and have been preached by many people down the ages, particularly in certain oriental religions, notably Buddhism, with its emphasis on the power of cause and effect.

These principles outlined here are in fact based on the laws of nature. However, we live in a society which is empirical, that is to say scientists will accept only what can be directly measured as 'truth'. Therefore, these essential principles are not fully appreciated by the vast majority of people, and are not generally taught at schools and universities, where they would for the most part be ridiculed as unscientific mumbo-jumbo. Nevertheless, they work, as people who use them will testify.

People don't get rid of debt and become happy and prosperous by accident or luck—they know what they want and they work to get it! We shall say more on this subject in the next section. In the meantime, it is worth summarizing what has already been stated, because it is so vitally important to your future success.

Points to Remember

● If you want to improve your situation you must adopt a positive mental attitude.

● You must strive constantly to improve your self-image, and thereby gain a positive mental attitude, by feeding your subconscious mind positive thoughts and images.

● The way to do this is to tell yourself morning and evening that you have your desired personal characteristics and that you will achieve your goals by the stated time. You do this by *visualizing* your desired objectives coming true.

● You must state clearly and concisely exactly what your goals are. They must be written down, in a place where you may easily refer to them. Set weekly and monthly goals, as well as long-term ones.

● You should also tell yourself that you *deserve* to achieve your goals, as this is a rapid way to overcome an inadequate self-image.

● Start with small goals, achieve those, and move on to bigger ones.

● Once you have begun to visualize a better life and to set specific goals, you must persist until you begin to see results. Once the first results have been achieved, you will need no further convincing.

STEP 3

Use the Power of the Subconscious

There is one final aspect of the subconscious mind which you must understand and use in order to get out of debt and prosper. The awesome *computing power* of the subconscious mind can—and must—be used for problem solving. So let's just think about the nature of problems for a minute.

There Will Always be Problems!

A vital, albeit obvious point to remember is that you will inevitably have problems from time to time. Maybe they won't seem or be as serious as those which face you now, but you can rest assured that problems in general will never disappear altogether. The problems may change their form: follow the programme outlined in this book and the problems of debt should soon become the problems of affluence, such as: 'How do I protect what I have managed to accumulate?' rather than: 'How do I accumulate enough cash to get out of debt?' Nevertheless, they will still be problems of a sort. The more you try to achieve, the more problems you will have. So embrace your problems—they are a sign that you are alive and kicking. Lots of problems can also mean lots of success, for it is a sure bet that however many problems you have had, they have come with successes as well.

A Problem is an Opportunity in Disguise

One of the most positive ways to view a problem is to see it as an opportunity in disguise. I only learned this fairly recently, and at first I scoffed at the notion. However, the longer certain apparently intransigent problems persisted in my life, the more I began to see them as opportunities.

One of the best examples I can think of is losing your job. At first this might be a great shock, accompanied by a lot of fear and worry, such as 'How can I pay the mortgage? Who will employ me at my age?', etc. These are all normal and even predictable reactions.

You can, however, choose to see losing your job as an opportunity. For example, if you had previously disliked your occupation, or had not particularly enjoyed it, you might see your new-found unemployment as an opportunity to find a profession which you might enjoy a great deal more. You might also choose to retrain for an entirely different way of life, one which suits your talents much better and brings you enjoyment.

Many people who have been fired or made redundant in high-unemployment areas have seen their dismissal as an opportunity to set up in business on their own doing things that they like. Take the town of Corby in Northamptonshire as an example. During the big recession of the early 1980s the steelworks shut down; overnight Corby became virtually a ghost town. Yet within a remarkably short space of time it had attracted new industries and actually has emerged today in a stronger, more diversified economic position.

At the other end of the scale, thousands of highly paid workers in the City of London's financial sector found themselves unemployed in the wake of the great stock-market crash of October 1987. This was a shock for them in view of the relatively high salaries many had been earning. Many subsequently found very different employment, and have reported that they enjoy life much more, and have a much better quality of life compensating for lower salaries. Few in this situation would voluntarily return to life in the City.

Other less dramatic problems may also be seen as opportunities. If you can't do something in a certain way, then quite probably the very impediment you are facing will become an opportunity. It is all a question of perspective.

A good way to change your perspective is to let your imagination run riot in a series of 'what if' scenarios. Take a pen and paper and write down all the various means of tackling the problem, or of changing the nature of the problem. Write them all down, no matter how apparently ludicrous. For example, suppose you need a part-time job to increase your income, and you are finding it hard to find opportunities. You could write, what if:

● I acted as an agent selling some useful household product to friends and relatives?

- I started a small business offering a necessary service to homes and businesses in the area, such as cleaning, gardening, child-minding?
- I approached the bosses of firms which are doing well in the area to ask about, or to suggest part-time work opportunities?
- I asked my firm for overtime work, even in a different area to that in which I normally work?
- I drove a mini-cab?
- I became a market researcher?
- I collected and sold unwanted goods at a car boot sale?
- I wrote articles for the local paper?

And so on—I'm sure you can think of lots of ideas. Don't worry if you do not get an immediate solution, you are providing a lot of creative material for your mind to work with.

Your Subconscious Computer

Think of your subconscious mind as a massive computer, a great deal more powerful and advanced than anything yet invented. As we have already seen, it synthesizes all the data stored in your brain, and produces staggering solutions to problems—some of which may appear intractable to the conscious mind. It is necessary to discover how to 'access' the computing power of the subconscious. In this way you will tap its amazing problem-solving potential to produce a debt-free, prosperous and happy existence.

It may seem contradictory, but the way to solve problems is to stop thinking consciously about them. Your subconscious mind can only really go to work when you stop the flow of conscious thoughts, many of them petty, mundane and repetitive. The method is simple, but requires quiet and concentration. The first thing you must do is to cut out all extraneous noise. Noise kills proper thought, distracting the brain from doing its clever work. You must find a quiet place to sit, away from all the noise. There is probably somewhere in your house, a spare room, a bedroom or an attic, where you can sit quietly.

Take the phone off the hook, get a relative to look after the children, do whatever you have to do to isolate yourself. Then sit quietly and stop thinking consciously by trying to think of nothing at all! You will find that some wax ear plugs are a great help—the type that can be bought very cheaply at your local chemist.

Thinking of nothing is not easy at first, but persist and you will get better at it. Concentrate on 'not thinking' one minute at a time. You will soon enjoy the feeling of release generated from this experience. It is extremely relaxing. You may even find yourself falling asleep. (This tendency should be avoided as far as possible!)

You will not get immediate answers to your problems. However, you are allowing the subconscious to do its work even more efficiently than before. More importantly, you are opening up channels for those thoughts to be expressed. After a while, you will start to get answers to your problems, even the most difficult, popping into your head. You will know that these answers are coming from the subconscious mind because they will 'feel right'. You will feel very strongly that you ought to put the idea into action straight away—even if it is something that you never remotely thought of as a solution before. Just such a subconscious thought prompted me to write this book. I immediately sat down and started writing, because I felt irresistibly impelled to do so.

As we have seen, the more you try to achieve in your life, the more problems you will face. However, they will start to become more manageable. Using your subconscious mind, you will find solutions leaping out at you at odd moments. Those solutions will be so exciting that you will be instantly keen to put them into action; and that is exactly what you must do. If you ignore the promptings of your subconscious, they will dry up for a while, as your 'third mind' goes into a sulk. Put your subconscious promptings into action without delay, because they *will* bring you results.

The amazing power of the subconscious mind, if programmed properly, is the reason I am so certain that even people who consider themselves to be utterly poverty-stricken and trapped in debt will be able to lift themselves up.

Most practitioners of the art of accessing the subconscious computer recommend doing so for twenty to thirty minutes every day. It doesn't really matter if you skip the odd day, but it is best to get into the regular habit of enjoying stillness and silence, and not thinking. Apart from being a very powerful problem-solving tool, accessing the subconscious mind is also very therapeutic and relaxing.

Another word for accessing the subconscious computer is meditating. Meditation has been shown in laboratory studies to reduce stress and increase stamina, work and conscious problem-solving capacity. Again, it is a method widely taught and practised in the East, but little understood or practised in Western countries. At school, and in particular in higher education, we are taught to use only our conscious, logical, left-brained method to solve problems. Yet complex problems like eradicating debt and increasing income cannot be left wholly to logic. Difficult problems have to be tackled in the holistic, right-brained fashion associated with the subconscious mind, which considers all the elements of a problem. Logical thinking is straight-line thinking, and can only deal with one element of a problem at a time.

The use of holistic problem-solving methods was pioneered in the West by Edward de Bono, among others. His methods are widely studied in large corporations, which pay fat fees for seminars and training courses on the subject. De Bono calls the use of the powers of the subconscious mind 'lateral thinking', which is to say that the solution you are searching for may not be obvious at the end of a linear thought process. It may demand instead a radical departure from the stodgy way of thinking which gave rise to the problem in the first place.

Solving Urgent Problems

We do not always have the luxury of time to satisfy urgent problems. If you have a problem which requires an urgent solution, you must use your subconscious mind to solve it for you quickly.

I have found that the best way to do this is as follows.

- Consider all the angles by committing possible solutions to paper, as discussed above.

- Set a deadline—ask your subconscious mind to come up with a solution by a certain date and time.

- Sit quietly and meditate for half an hour or so. Try as far as possible to think of nothing, and certainly not to think of your pressing problem.

- Forget about your problem until the deadline arrives, at which time the solution will come to you.

Often a solution will be found after an overnight sleep, when you awake refreshed in the morning. Your subconscious mind doesn't go to sleep, it keeps working on the problem until a solution is found. Hence the source of the popular saying: 'I'll sleep on it', which people often say when they are faced with a difficult decision.

It is very important for you not to think consciously about the problem once you have handed it over to your subconscious to solve.

Let your subconscious mind do its job, and don't clutter it up with conscious thoughts. One other thing to note is that many of the answers handed to you by your subconscious will seem blindingly simple and obvious, if perhaps a bit ambitious. You may ask yourself 'why didn't I think of that before?' The answer is, of course, that you weren't using your subconscious mind before!

One of the first times I needed to use this method was when I was about to embark on a consultancy job which meant that I had to travel abroad for a month. Less than 24 hours before I was due to leave, another client rang up and offered me lucrative work on a training course, due to start the day after I was scheduled to return from my job abroad. The only problem was, the course required a lot of preparation and there was no way I could do it while I was away.

I said I would call back the following day. For the life of me, I couldn't think of a solution to the problem of having to do two jobs at once. I gave the problem to my subconscious mind to solve, with a deadline of 8 a.m. the following morning.

Sure enough, the answer came. My subconscious mind 'told' me to employ an assistant to compile the necessary teaching material while I was away, and also told me exactly whom to employ. I was able to arrange for this to be done, and the person chosen did an excellent job. I collected the material upon my return, and the training course was pronounced a great success.

In case you think that the solution to my problem was obvious, I can assure you that to me at the time it was not, at least not until my subconscious mind came up with the answer. This was one of the first times I had deliberately used the powers of my subconscious to solve a pressing problem, and I was astounded at the results.

Most of the time, our problems are persistent, but not so pressing that they require immediate solutions. Under these circumstances, solutions will come to you at odd times, often when you are doing nothing in particular, such as washing up or taking the dog for a walk. When they do, you will be transfixed, and eager to jump into action.

Keeping a Record

Most people do not have a photographic memory—I certainly don't. When you are meditating in peace and quiet, inspirations and understandings about yourself will flash through your head. When they do, you will want to record them for future use. All of the inspirations and aspects of self-knowledge which come to you in this way are important, but perhaps may not be immediately applicable or useful. So you will need to record them.

For this purpose it is wise to keep a special notebook. It may well be the one in which you have written down your plans, goals and characteristics necessary for success. If you also record the special, vital thoughts you have had while meditating you will be building up a valuable data bank for future use. You can either write them up as they come to you or immediately after you have finished meditating for the day.

Get the Action Habit

You may still be in a state of shock at the extent of your debt burden and your related personal problems. It may be difficult for you to believe that you will develop answers to your problems. You do, however, have a great deal of emotion about your circumstances, though, and a burning desire to improve them. This will help you to get results quickly. It is not enough merely to say that you want to achieve a certain characteristic or material possession. You must feel and visualize that situation. Remember that it is the thought *mixed with emotion* that produces results. Right now, you have plenty of emotion!

In order to prove what I am saying, you must take *action*. You have, of course, read and absorbed the information given here, but once you have done that you must move to put the lessons into practice. For example, you might agree that setting goals is a good idea, but you must now take the time to do it.

Even if you really mean to begin the programme, or any other action which your subconscious mind has prompted you to do, it can be hard to get yourself moving. It is easy to delay, or to find excuses. There are two simple ways to deal with such procrastination:

● Set a deadline.
● Start working automatically.

If I am 'cold calling', where I have to go and introduce complete strangers to my products and services, I set a time and just start doing it. If I am writing, I do the same and type anything that comes into my head, sorting out the order and detail later. The important thing is to make a start, until you find your natural rhythm and begin to enjoy what you are doing. The more you do, the more benefits you will get. So start *today!*

Face Your Fear

Perhaps the biggest obstacle you will have to face—bigger even than low self-confidence—is fear. Your new goals imply risk-taking, and getting out of your comfortable rut. This can be quite scary: better the devil you know, you may think. However, unless you learn to face your fear, you will take no action to alleviate your situation.

There is no shame in being afraid to do something; you should only be ashamed if you do nothing. The way to deal with fear is through action. Fear must not be allowed to paralyze you.

The simple truth is that action conquers fear. If you are consumed with worry and unease, the only solution is going to be action directed against that fear. Taking positive action will reduce the level of uncertainty and financial paralysis that is plaguing your life. So we come back to the action principle: *do it now!*

The Power of Persistence

The road to success and a life free from debt is not always smooth. All sorts of problems arise—in fact by definition, the more you try to accomplish, the more difficulties you will face. It is often the case that the most severe tests occur just before the moment of breakthrough.

If anything marks out the success from the failure, it is the quality of persistence. Anyone who is persistent will overcome obstacles on the way to success. If you have suffered great setbacks in the past, and have perhaps given way before them, then I would suggest that there is a good reason for this state of affairs. In the past, you were quite probably following the dictates of your conscious mind. You are now equipped to listen to your subconscious mind. Remember, the subconscious mind will always find a way out of your difficulties, in ways that you simply will not find through the use of the conscious mind. If difficulties cannot be overcome directly, the subconscious will find a way to go around them.

Failure responds to persistence. But persistence must be intelligent! If your first plan doesn't quite work, try another. If that doesn't do the trick, try yet another. In this way, you will gradually hone your efforts, achieving a laser-like focus until you discover exactly how to overcome your problems. Unintelligent persistence—whereby you stubbornly refuse to modify your plans to suit new circumstances, or to overcome failure, will result in more disheartening failure. Stop, listen to the inner voice of your subconscious, modify your approach, and try again. Keep trying until failure gives up on you.

There are lots of examples of the power of persistence. My favourite concerns Thomas Edison, who made 1000 attempts before he managed to create the first electric light bulb. He did not refer to his unsuccessful attempts as 'failures', but as 'ways that it wouldn't work'.

A more recent example concerns Tracey Edwards, the first woman to captain a boat with an all-woman crew in the round-the-world Whitbread yacht race. She faced innumerable difficulties in her efforts to find a boat and raise the money to restore and equip it. To top it all she had to approach 300 potential sponsors before finding a backer only weeks before the race was due to begin. Needless to say, Tracey and her crew did extremely well, coming second overall in their boat's class. There are many such stories of the rewards of persistence, both on a large and small scale, and we can read about them virtually every day in newspapers and magazines.

Of all the basic principles of success in any endeavour, persistence is probably the hardest taskmaster. However, in return for persistence, you are guaranteed success. Just make sure that your persistence is based on a firm foundation of realistic plans, earnest desire, keen focus, and the dictates of your subconscious mind. As long as this is the case, failure will eventually give up on you.

Peer Pressure

It is a curious trait of social groups that when an individual tries to break out of his or her circumstances, the others in the group will try to prevent the change from happening. A group has cohesion because all of its members are like each other. Your friends are for the most part bound to be like you. If you are heavily in debt, or in a low-income job, or both, then the chances are that your friends will be in similar circumstances.

Consider what is likely to happen when an individual starts to leave the group, to enter a better material situation. Will the individual be applauded or encouraged by those around him or her? Not likely! The opposite will happen—he or she will be chastized for trying to be different.

If you are determined to improve your lot in life, many of your so-called friends may disappear. You will be developing at a rapid rate; while they are static. Only a few are likely to remain your friends, and you may find that you have less in common with them than was previously the case. As you start to move in the direction of prosperity, many people will disparage what you are trying to achieve. They may be openly scornful or even worse, as the poet Alexander Pope put it, they may 'Damn with faint praise'. When you relaunch your career, or start a new venture, lots of timid souls will say that they 'hope it works', while their tone of voice will inform you that they don't expect it to. Some will express their negativity in even stronger terms.

Even those closest to you may behave in this manner—your partner, sister or brother, mother and father, or your best friend. At bottom, such an attitude is born not of concern for your welfare, but out of fear of losing you. The fear is of course justified, at least for those people who refuse to take risks or to attempt a similar self-improvement programme. In the meantime, you will have to deal with negativity openly or covertly expressed. I have found it useful not to be too open about my plans, but to demonstrate by results. If people tell you that they think you are barmy or bound to fail, then you must firmly tell them that you are in control of your fate, and that you would appreciate it if they kept their thoughts to themselves. Most people will give way to your point of view if you show enough confidence.

Once you are on the way to showing results, your nearest and dearest may start copying you! If they do, you could save them at lot of time by giving them the benefit of the information you've gleaned from this book.

Points to Remember

- Stop trying to solve your problems using only your conscious mind. You must learn to use the power of the subconscious mind.

- Access your subconscious computer through the practice of meditation. Set a time and a place each day to empty your mind of everyday thoughts and try to think of nothing at all.

- Subconscious truths will come to you as a series of hunches or inspirations. Put them into practice immediately, or at least record them for future use.

- If you have an urgent problem, try to think consciously of possible solutions, recording them on paper. Meditate as usual, then set a deadline for the subconscious mind to produce a solution. Ignore the problem until the deadline is reached.

- Don't hesitate to put subconscious solutions into practice when the time is right. Be bold when you feel that the solution is correct. Get into the action habit, pushing fear away.

- Remember the power of persistence. Make a point of learning from people who have overcome their difficulties and have achieved extraordinary success.

- Guard against negative thinking from others. People around you may try to belittle your attempts to get out of debt in an unconscious attempt to keep you at their own level. Strive to go your own way in life.

PART 2

Getting Out of Debt

Annual income twenty pounds, annual expenditure nineteen, nineteen six, result happiness. Annual income twenty pounds, annual expenditure twenty pounds ought and six, result misery.

— Mr Micawber, in *David Copperfield* by Charles Dickens.

STEP 4

Understand the Cost of Debt

To gain control of your personal finances, it is absolutely vital to understand exactly where the money you earn goes. Many people have only a hazy idea of the pattern of their expenditure, and few stop to think about what all those mortgages, bank loans and outstanding credit card balances actually cost in hard cash. If you haven't yet bothered to work this out I can guarantee that the results will surprise, if not shock you.

Once you understand the mathematics of debt you can work your way out of the debt treadmill and eventually 'play the system' to accumulate wealth. The mathematics of debt are probably working against you at present, but they *can* be harnessed to work for you. Taking the time to understand debt now will pay financial dividends in the future.

For this section, you will find it helpful to keep a pen and paper handy, and also a pocket calculator, so you can see how debt works. We will begin by looking at what interest is, how interest rates are determined, and how they are measured.

What Determines Interest Rates?

Interest is quite simply the rent you pay for the use of someone else's money. It is dependent upon a complex mix of forces governing supply and demand locally, nationally and internationally. At this point you might like to note that interest rates throughout the 1980s and early 1990s have been at levels which are, historically speaking, exceptionally high. During the 1950s and 1960s, for example, you could borrow money at 4 or 5 per cent per annum, whereas in the late 1980s/early 1990s the cost was more likely to have been upwards of 16 per cent.

The lowest lending rates chargeable by UK banks in sterling are decided by the Chancellor of the Exchequer, and imposed by the UK's central bank, the Bank of England. The Chancellor fixes a minimum lending rate, also known as the base rate, and which rises and falls depending on international conditions and national policies. The banks in turn fix a prime lending rate, which is usually a little above the base rate, and is the measure by which credit is given.

The prime lending rate in the late 1980s/early 1990s has been much higher in the UK than in other industrialized countries, which is an indication of the relative weakness of the British economy. For example, in 1990 the prime lending rate in the US was 10 per cent; West Germany's was 10.5 per cent; Japan's 8 per cent, while the UK's was 15 per cent. Weaker economies, such as that of Australia, have had to offer even higher interest rates to attract foreign funds and to contain inflationary demand at home: in Australia, the prime lending rate in 1990 was as high as 19 per cent.

Interest rates in countries like the US and West Germany—often described as 'locomotives of the world economy'—are of the utmost importance to British domestic rates. If the US puts its rates up to maintain the confidence of foreign investors, you can usually be sure that British rates will follow suit before long. The interest rate differential between countries reflects the different degrees of risk associated with investing in their different economies. In some countries, such as Switzerland, where investment is considered to be an extremely small risk, the returns to investment will be very low, or even negative. In other words, when people are worried about the safety of their money in the US or the UK, and deposit it in Switzerland, they may actually have to pay for the privilege of placing their cash with Swiss banks.

The different degrees of risk associated with investment in different countries are paralleled by different degrees of risk in lending to consumers within a country. Banks lend to each other at low rates of interest, close to the base rate. Often they will use the London Interbank Offer Rate (LIBOR) as a yardstick for lending to other institutions. Big blue-chip companies like ICI might be able to borrow money at only one percentage point above LIBOR. They may then re-lend the money (to a credit card company, for example) at a higher interest rate, and so make a profit.

The more the likelihood of default, the higher the interest rate. That is one of the reasons why credit cards are so expensive. Issuers of Access and Visa cards know that about 3 per cent of the holders will default, and build this into their profit calculations. If, on the other hand, they can issue cards only to less risky consumers, such as high-income earners, then they can reduce the interest rate payable. Holders of 'gold cards' tend to earn large salaries and are considered good risks; therefore they can borrow money at nearly half the rate charged to 'ordinary' credit-card recipients.

The Flat Rate vs the Annual Percentage Rate (APR)

There are three ways of measuring interest rates. Not long ago, the conventional method was to quote a flat rate. A flat rate simply describes what percentage of the loan the lender must be repaid over a given period. For example, in April 1990 Midland bank offered loans of over £500 or more at a flat rate of 12 per cent annually.

However, because interest is usually charged monthly on the outstanding balance, the true annual rate will be much higher. The actual interest paid as a percentage of a 12 per cent flat rate loan will be 23.8 per cent by the end of the year. This is known as the Annual Percentage Rate, or APR. Since 1982 the APR has by law been stated alongside any loans offered. So no one has an excuse not to understand the real cost of borrowing!

Sometimes you may see an annual rate quoted on a loan which is simply an aggregate of the monthly interest rate, for example, if a credit card charges 1.9 per cent per month, this could be quoted as an apparent annual rate of 22.8 per cent (1.9 multiplied by 12). However, the APR will actually be higher, at 25.3 per cent.

The Power of Compound Interest

The difference between the flat rate and the Annual Percentage Rate on loans calculated monthly, or even daily, demonstrates the power of *compound interest*. Compounding means calculating the interest on the interest. For example, suppose that you borrow £100 on a credit card at an interest rate of 2 per cent per month. At the end of the first month you owe the company £102. Next month, you do not pay interest only on the original £100 borrowed, but on the new figure of £102. So at the end of the second month you owe the credit card company £102 x 2 per cent / £2.04. Adding this to the original £102 increases the debt to £104.04 at the end of the second month.

This may not sound like a big difference in the early months or years, but over time the compounding factor accelerates the growth of your debt. After a year you will owe £124.34; after five years £321.67. If you would like to calculate what compound interest will do to your own debts, a simple formula and an example are given in Appendix 3.

To take a much larger example, the power of compound interest explains why so many countries cannot repay their debts to British banks, no matter how hard they try. Countries like Brazil and Argentina, which owe in excess of $60 billion each, are still paying off the *interest* on their debts. Since few of them manage to pay more than the extra interest added to their debt each year, their debt burdens inevitably grow.

The power of compound interest to make a sum of money grow has sometimes been called the 'eighth wonder of the world'. One of the most famous examples to illustrate this power concerns Manhattan Island. In 1726 the Dutch purchased Manhattan from the American Indian tribe living there. The sum paid was the equivalent only of £15. If this money had been invested at an interest rate of 8 per cent annually, and the proceeds continually reinvested, the final figure today would exceed the value of land and property on the entire island of Manhattan.

If you cannot envisage accumulating that much wealth over such a long period, then consider this example. A sum of £40,000 invested at a compound rate of only 7 per cent annually will make you a millionaire in 50 years!

There is more about the almost magical properties of compound interest in Chapter 10, where we will consider the importance of getting into the savings habit. For now, it should be sufficient to note that as a debtor, the power of compound interest is working against you. Once you have dumped your debt and begun saving, it will instead begin to work in your favour, with dramatic results.

What Credit Cards Cost You

Storecards

The costs of credit card debt can vary considerably. At the top end of the range of these self-imposed financial millstones are storecards, which charge very high rates of interest. For example, Marks and Spencer's Chargecard, charged a monthly rate of 2.5 per cent in 1990, giving an APR of 34.5 per cent. Credit cards from high street multiples like Dixons and Comet cost even more, at 36 per cent APR. No wonder these stores encourage you to use their 'instant credit'—it can add one third to the price of their 'discount' goods.

Standard Credit Cards

In the middle of the range are the everyday Access and Visa cards, which in 1990 charged around 1.9 to 2.3 per cent monthly. Lloyds Access charged 1.9 per cent a month, giving an APR of 25.3 per cent. However, Midland charged 2.35 per cent monthly, pushing the APR up to 32.1 per cent.

You might think that Visa and Access interest rates would be the same for account holders, when in fact they vary from bank to bank. Perhaps you are holding both types of card. You might not notice that it costs an extra £17 a year to buy £1,000 worth of goods with a card charging only an extra 0.1 per cent a month interest. However, if you buy £1000 worth of stereo equipment from a shop like Comet using its storecard, then you will pay an extra £84 over and above what Lloyds Access charges.

You can see why many chainstores won't accept other credit cards. They are making up to 33 per cent more a month on outstanding balances than they would if they allowed you to pay by Visa or Access.

Preferential Interest Rate Cards

The next-lowest interest rates are those charged on cards issued by banks and offered to people whose credit record is good. These might only charge only a few percentage points above the base rate. The cheapest plastic credit of all is available to 'gold card' holders, who are high earners (in the £25,000 to £30,000 a year or more bracket). Usually, they can borrow up to £10,000 at attractive rates only 2 to 3 per cent or so above the base rate. In 1990 Gold Card holders were charged as little as 18.7 per cent APR for their outstanding credit card debt. This is around one third less than that payable by holders of Access or Visa cards.

Table 1: Examples of Credit Card Interest Rates (1990)

Issuer	Monthly interest rate	APR	Cost of £1,000
Storecards			
Marks and Spencer	2.5	34.5	£345
Dixons	2.6	36.0	£360
Comet	2.6	36.0	£360

Table 1:   Examples of Credit Card Interest Rates (1990) (cont)

Issuer	Monthly interest rate	APR	Cost of £1,000
Other			
Midland	2.35	32.1	£321
TSB Trustcard	2.3	31.3	£313
Bank of Scotland	2.2	29.8	£298
Lloyds	1.9	25.3	£253
Barclaycard	1.85	24.6	£246
Preferential interest cards			
American Express Optima	1.6	21.8	£218
Lloyds Goldcard	1.6	22.4	£224
Barclays Premier Card	1.3	18.7	£187

Table 1 is not an exhaustive list of credit cards available. It illustrates the point I have been making—there is a big range in the rates of interest charged to customers, both between stores and banks, and between types of customers. To find out what percentage interest you are paying annually on your credit card, simply multiply the outstanding amount by the APR, then divide by 100.

It is important to note also that the cards charging the lowest fees also tend to charge a membership fee, ranging from around £6 to £15 annually. Of course, this fee increases the costs of borrowing, but it compensates the banks for those tiresome customers who insist on paying off their credit card balances in full each month. Otherwise, the banks would not make any money out of these financially-aware individuals.

What if You Just Pay the Minimum?

One of the least understood aspects of payment by credit card is the length of time it takes to pay for your goods if you only repay the minimum 5 per cent monthly on the outstanding balance. If we assume that you have the cheapest ordinary credit card in the table above, which is Lloyds Access or Barclaycard, incurring interest charges of 1.9 per cent per month on a charge of £1000, and are paying the minimum each month, then it will take *eight years* to repay the balance.

Table 2 gives an example. Borrowing £1,000 at an interest rate of 1.9 per cent monthly means that after 7 years and 11 months of regular minimum payments of the outstanding balance you will have paid off the loan. The total amount of interest paid to the credit card company will have been £560.87. So you will have made payments of more than half the original amount on top of the loan. If we assume that you do not hang on until the bitter end, and clear the balance after, say four years, you will have paid total interest of £469.54 on the money borrowed—a premium of almost half.

Table 2: Costs of Borrowing £1,000 at 1.9 per cent Monthly Interest, Repaying at the Minimum Permitted Monthly Sum

Month	Balance	Cumulative Interest paid
0	£1,000.00	0.00
12	677.29	191.91
24	458.72	321.89
36	310.69	409.92
48	210.42	469.54
60	142.52	509.92
72	94.63	537.27
84	51.92	554.56
95	0.00	560.87

To calculate how long it will take you to repay your credit card debt, multiply the balance by the monthly interest rate, and then deduct the minimum payment. You may well have to carry out this exercise for a long time before you reach zero. Remember also that our example assumes that the debtor is using a credit card offering a moderate rate of interest. If a storecard is used, then the interest rate is likely to be at least 25 per cent greater, which means that it takes even longer to pay off the loan by making minimum monthly payments—nine and a half years, to be precise.

Worse than this, compulsive credit card spenders keep using their plastic, adding to the monthly balance, and ensuring that past purchases continue to attract high rates of interest, as the balance does not get reduced.

To summarize—*you must pay off your credit card debts as a priority*. You should only use credit cards as convenient purchasing tools to replace cash at the moment of purchase, paying the balance at the end of each month and incurring no interest rate charges. If you absolutely have to have credit (and I don't believe this is ever the case) then you should shop around. Even if you don't qualify as a 'gold card' holder (and most of us do not), you can pay over one third less if you use an ordinary card rather than a storecard.

However, if you are using any type of credit card, and are failing to repay in full each month, then you really have two options: Either incinerate your cards or cut them up into little pieces! That way you'll almost certainly save yourself hundreds, if not thousands of pounds over the years.

The Cost of Bank Loans

Bank loans are not usually as expensive as credit-cards as a means of borrowing, and are supposed to have the advantage over credit cards in that they can give you cash with which you may bargain to obtain discounts—especially on major purchases like cars. However, remember that interest will more than eat up your discount. Interest rates offered on personal bank loans are competitive between lenders. Yet there are still differences to be found.

Table 3:   Bank Loan Rates (1990)

Cost of £1,000 loan

Lender	APR	1yr	3yrs	5yrs
Lloyds	25.3	£127.76	£389.96	£684.80
Barclays	24.4	£123.32	£375.56	£658.40
Nat West	27.4	£137.36	£421.28	£742.40
Midland	25.8	£130.00	£390.00	—
Midland	24.1	—	—	£650.00

Table 3 calculates the total amount repaid minus the amount borrowed to show the total interest charged over different time periods. As we can see, the cost of borrowing £1000 from each of the 'big four' banks varies. The 'spread' (the difference between the highest and lowest quotes) rises from £14.04 for a loan over 12 months, to £45.72 over three years, and to £92.40 over a five year period.

Remember that these rates are for loans for which you are not incurring *loan repayment insurance*—the premium added to the amount of your loan to ensure that if you die, become incapacitated or are involuntarily unemployed, your loan will continue to be repaid by the insurance company. Repayment insurance is actively encouraged by the banks to reduce the risks attached to lending, protecting them from the threat of default. It also adds to profits where the banks are themselves underwriting the insurance. If you accept the loan repayment insurance premium, the annual cost increases. Insurance premiums in 1990 for the big four banks in this example are given in Table 4:

Table 4

	1yr	3yrs	5yrs
Lloyds	£67.00	£101.00	£183.00
Barclays	£66.87	£126.79	£189.12
Nat West	£64.00	£98.00	£161.00
Midland	£71.00	£106.00	£184.00

In this comparison Barclays charges the lowest APR but the highest insurance premiums, reducing the price differential between its loans and those of its competitors. Nat West charges the highest interest rate but the lowest insurance premiums.

Thus the differential between the highest and lowest charges among the big four banks rises from £11.17 for a £1,000 loan over one year, to £28.32 over three years, and to £69.40 over five years. This is not to say that the differentials in loan rates charged between banks are fixed—on the contrary, they are constantly changing.

Some banks also offer permanent loan facilities known as cashflow accounts, where you elect to pay a set amount each month into an account. In return, you receive an overdraft facility of up to 30 times the monthly sum paid. This form of bank lending is more insidious than a straightforward bank loan, since you can enter the never-ending chain of debt where you keep using the cheque book to add more purchases to the outstanding balance.

A cashflow account is very similar to a credit card account in its encouragement for the holder constantly to spend the outstanding credit balance. In calculating the cost of a cashflow account, therefore, you should use the method already described for assessing the cost of credit card debt.

Another common form of bank lending is an overdraft. These are sometimes encouraged by banks, who offer a more or less permanent overdraft facility to many of their customers. The limit will depend upon your income, credit history, and the length of time over which you have had an account with the bank. An overdraft is repayable at any time, so if your bank manager believes that you are in financial trouble he could demand immediate repayment.

The cost of an overdraft will be similar to that of a cashflow account. Added costs will be account charges which are automatically enforced when you overdraw, yet which you would otherwise probably not have to pay. So the cost of maintaining an average monthly overdraft of £500 will not only be the 20 per cent or so you pay in interest annually, but the considerable account charges levied on all your deposits and withdrawals, whether or not your account was in credit at the time.

Regardless of the type of bank loan you get, the costs of borrowing cash over a period of, say, three to five years are high. You will end up repaying at a minimum between 40 and 70 per cent of the loan amount as interest over the chosen period. Only short-term loans of a year or less offer apparently cheap repayment terms.

If you feel that you must borrow from a bank, which is still preferable to borrowing with a credit card, the message is clear. Shop around for the best deal and keep the borrowing period as short as possible.

The bank loans discussed above are unsecured loans, which means that you are not required to indemnify yourself with a charge against your property (i.e.:agree to sell your home in the event of default). It does not mean, however, that a bank cannot force you to pay up. It just takes a bit longer when you have not formally secured the loan against your home or other assets. But do not panic if you are in this situation, bank managers are human, and will make a reasonable settlement if you are honest about your financial distress; unlike some of the characters discussed below.

Secured Loans

During the 1980s, a subsector of the financial services industry gained new respectability. These were the companies advertising in the local newspapers offering instant cash over telephone hotlines. We were exhorted to 'pay off all credit card bills and consolidate them in one loan at a lower interest rate'. This is only worth considering *if you pay off the credit card balances in full, and cancel the agreements.* If you don't do this, the chances are that you will begin to use your credit cards again and that you will run up another huge bill, and get into an even worse situation.

It will be shown in the next few chapters that there is another way. It is far better to pay off old debt steadily by living within your means.

Companies offering loans at lower interest rates than those charged by the banks do so for two reasons. Firstly, you are encouraged to take out a loan over a long period, often over five years or more, and sometimes over ten to fifteen years. This means that you are locked into high fixed-interest payments, regardless of what happens to the base rate over that long period. There is a good chance that rates will come down in the 1990s, leaving you paying through the nose for past 'cheap' credit. Secondly, the loans are secured on your home, which means that the finance company can force you to sell it if you fall behind on the payments.

Unsurprisingly, secured loan rates vary a lot. You can pay as little as 14.6 per cent for a large loan (usually £7,500 or more), or as much as 20.9 per cent for a smaller loan. In the latter case, it might seem a bit silly to take out a secured loan when you can get an unsecured bank loan for less. On the other hand, if you are already considered a credit risk by a bank, a secured loan might be your only alternative. However, you would still be better off foregoing that fitted kitchen for a less indebted standard of living.

Unlicensed Credit Brokers

At the bottom of the scale of lenders are those who are not licensed by the government, and whose activities it is therefore difficult to regulate. Unlicensed credit brokers will lend to high risk groups of people, who naturally pay very high interest rates for the loans. Companies offering such facilities vary from being responsible and above board to back-street loan sharks.

Many unlicensed credit brokers will waste no time in harassing or prosecuting you if you can't pay. Unfortunately, the one group of people who are least able to pay when they get into difficulties, i.e. the least creditworthy, are the ones forced into the arms of the loan sharks. Often, they are less well-informed than the mainstream debtor. Consequently, they tend to end up paying through the nose for credit.

Loan shark interest rates have much in common with those other loan sharks—people who offer store credit. If you are desperate enough to have fallen into the hands of these people, then you really do need to take stock of and tackle your problems without borrowing further.

What to Do if You Are in Trouble

It's best to get some credit counselling, through your local Citizen's Advice Bureau if you do not feel able to tackle your problems without assistance. You must not take the route of trying to borrow your way out of trouble when over-borrowing got you into this state in the first place, this really would be adding fuel to the fire. Your problems are never so desperate that they cannot be resolved by facing up to the facts and taking immediate action.

Resist threats by writing to the company and explaining the situation. Methods of dealing with creditors are discussed fully in Step 6. For now, don't panic about being taken to court by unlicensed credit brokers. The law is likely to take your side if you are making genuine attempts to get out of debt.

If violence has been threatened, then take the matter to the police without delay. The law has powers to deal with loan sharks who threaten violence.

The Cost of Mortgages

Mortgages do not, in most cases, charge a flat rate of interest, but a variable rate, which rises and falls in line with decisions made by both the Chancellor of the Exchequer and the building societies and banks. And interest is charged on the balance, not on the whole amount. With a conventional repayment mortgage, the repayments consist of both capital and interest. During the early years, only a small part of the repayments you make consist of the principal (capital), most is repayment of interest. Only in the later years of the repayment term do you start to pay off substantial chunks of the principal.

Over the term of a mortgage, your actual payments will come to a sum considerably larger than that borrowed, despite tax relief on the first £30,000. This is illustrated in Table 5. The first £30,000 borrowed at interest rates current in 1990 (15 per cent) repaid over 25 years, (which is the conventional length of time for repayment), comes to £90,720, which is more than three times the sum borrowed. Any further sums borrowed do not attract tax relief, so the multiple of principal repaid grows. For example, if you borrow another £30,000 at 15.0 per cent, you will end up repaying £116,010 which is nearly four times the principal. Clearly, the magic of compound interest will cost you dearly under these circumstances. If you go overboard and borrow £100,000 or more, the repayments will end up costing you well over three and a half times the initial sum borrowed.

Table 5

Principal	Sum repaid	Multiple of principal
£ 30,000	£ 90,720	3.02
£ 40,000	£129,390	3.23
£ 50,000	£168,060	3.36
£ 60,000	£206,730	3.45
£ 70,000	£245,400	3.51
£ 80,000	£284,070	3.55
£ 90,000	£322,740	3.59
£100,000	£361,410	3.61
£150,000	£554,760	3.70

At this point it will suffice to say that you do not have to suffer the burden of repaying an apparently endless mortgage. Step 7 considers ways of reducing the repayment burden. For now, you need only be aware of the real cost of a mortgage in hard cash.

Questions to Ask Lenders

If you are contemplating taking on a line of credit, or have taken one and are not sure of the terms, remember to ask these basic questions before proceeding:

- What is the Annual Percentage Rate of the loan?
- How much will the loan cost in total, including any repayment insurance premiums?
- Is the loan to be secured on your home or other assets?
- What procedure will be followed if you are unable to meet the repayments during the period of the loan?
- Who is the actual lender?
- Is the intermediary (the person offering you the loan) registered by the government with FIMBRA (The Financial Intermediaries, Managers and Brokers Association)?

Points to Remember

- Interest rates in 1990 have been at their highest in living memory. High interest rates reflect real economic weaknesses worldwide, and in the UK in particular.

- Your debts are accumulated on the basis of compound interest. This means you pay interest on the interest!
- Compound interest is a tremendously powerful force. It causes your debts to accelerate over time.
- Credit cards are expensive if you do not pay off the full balance by the due date.
- Avoid storecards which charge the highest rates of interest. All credit cards should be destroyed if debt is becoming a problem for you.
- Understand the hidden costs of bank loans, and the variation in rates between lenders.
- If you are in the hands of loan sharks, get professional help immediately.
- Understand that if you default on a secured loan you are in danger of losing your home.
- Find out what your mortgage really costs you if you repay over a conventional period of time.
- Take the time to understand fully what each of your debts costs you.

STEP 5

Find Out Where the Money Goes

You will recognize from the outset that in order to eliminate your debt you will not only need to understand the mathematics of debt, but you will also need to plan your spending. However, in order to plan your spending, you need to know *exactly* how much you spend, and on what.

Very few people know precisely how much they spend monthly, quarterly, or annually on the necessities and luxuries of life. You know how much your rent or mortgage payments are each month, but I'll bet you haven't much idea of the amount you spend on such things as newspapers, clothes, alcohol, cigarettes, bus fares, cinema tickets, sweets, snacks, groceries, petrol, oil, car parking fees, stationery, stamps, books, repairs, presents, sports, holidays, insurance and all the myriad other goods and services you require in order not just to survive, but to make your life bearable and fun.

When I first attempted to get out of debt, I made an effort to estimate many of these costs when designing a budget. The trouble was, I rarely had a clue how much I was actually spending on these odds and ends. I would also find that I kept overestimating or underestimating various categories of expenditure. Some things I forgot about altogether, particularly emergencies, such as having the car repaired, or needing the bathroom roof fixed.

Fortunately, I stumbled across an extremely simple but very exact method for understanding where my money went.

Every single time you make a purchase, of whatever kind or for whatever amount, you must record it. Carry around one of those little notebooks you can get in any stationers. When you make a purchase, record it. But don't think to yourself: 'Oh, I'll do it later, when I get home'. Record it there and then, and by the end of the day, you will have a spending record which looks like the one in Table 6:

Table 6:

Newspaper —	30p
Chocolate bar —	22p
10 stamps —	£2.20
Groceries —	£3.40
Petrol —	£10.50
Phone call —	20p
Total	**£16.82**

Two results will be gained from this exercise, which is surprisingly satisfying to do. In the first place you are likely to be amazed at the amount of money you spend. In the second place, you will never again be able to say that you have no idea where your money goes—you will know exactly!

Analysing Your Spending

Once you have begun to record your expenditure on a daily basis, you will then need to divide up your spending record into categories. Many categories are obvious, but you might like to use sub-categories to enable you to analyse your spending more carefully.

For example, *food* might be divided up into meat, vegetables, fruit, sweets and biscuits, etc. *Car* might be sub-categorized as petrol, oil, tax, spare parts, cleaning and so on. In this way, you will be able to identify exactly where you might make savings, or control your spending without losing your quality of life.

Let me give you a personal example. I love reading, and I used to be a terror in a bookshop, credit card in hand. I discovered that I was spending a small fortune on buying books, and almost as much on newspapers and magazines. I thought hard about what I read and why, and decided what I needed, and what I could do without.

The result was that I cut down on my purchase of my favourite and most expensive newspaper, to the one or two times a week when I could read and enjoy it most. I stopped buying magazines, because I hardly ever read them. Now they are reserved as a special treat for when I have the time—when on holiday, for example. I cut my book purchases dramatically by the simple expedient of destroying my credit cards and not spending as much time in bookshops as before. I rejoined our local library and started using it, which was good for catching up on newspapers and magazines as well as books. I also joined a book club, so that I could treat myself to a few titles a year, for which I was able to budget.

Another major category of my luxury spending was restaurants. Again, I dealt with this first by destroying my credit cards, and secondly by planning my visits to restaurants. My wife and I discovered some superb but moderately priced places to eat on those occasions when we felt we deserved a night out. Also, by paying cash, we found that we would be less tempted to overspend. Cash is real money to your subconscious mind, whereas a credit card slip is not. Of course, we found ourselves eating in much more than usual, but we worked at enlivening the experience by trying out more exciting dishes and treating ourselves to an occasional good bottle of wine. We also found on those occasions that we did go out that we could cut the restaurant bill down to size by leaving out the trimmings, like drinks before and coffee afterwards. We even found an excellent pasta restaurant in the middle of London's trendy West End where we could eat quite adequately and enjoyably for under £10 between us! The idea is not to stop enjoying life, but to keep one's spending on luxuries down to manageable proportions.

Monitoring your spending will reveal your indulgences starkly and often painfully. Once you have kept a daily record, you will be able to construct monthly, quarterly records, and annual records. They can be compiled simply, using ordinary lined paper, and with sub-totals underlined. Otherwise, you may wish to use an accounts book, which is already divided into columns, and which you can buy from a newsagent.

An example of a quarterly spending record is given in Table 7. The categories you invent to monitor your spending habits are up to you, as is the degree of detail you want to go into. However, as a general rule, the more detail the better, as it will help you all the more to analyze and plan your spending. Most people are likely to have around 35 to 40 categories of expenditure.

This example is fictitious, used for the purposes of illustration. However, it can immediately be seen that savings could be made in a number of areas, without prejudicing one's quality of life. Alcohol consumption could be cut down, for example, and the car could either be disposed of or used less often. Meat consumption could be reduced, and vegetable and fruit intake increased. Also, January is obviously a month of heavy expenditure, for which provision would have to be made throughout the rest of the year.

Table 7:   Example of a Spending Record

	January £	February £	March £	Total £
Household				
Poll Tax	35.00	35.00	35.00	105.00
Electricity	—	—	32.49	32.49
Gas	28.41	—	—	28.41
Telephone	—	43.72	—	43.72
Repairs/cleaning	15.00	23.50	8.40	46.90
Furniture	159.99	—	—	159.99
TV	—	60.00	—	60.00
Insurance	145.00	—	—	145.00
Sub total	**840.75**	**619.57**	**533.24**	**1,993.56**
Groceries				
Meat/poultry	18.68	19.23	20.14	58.05
Vegetables	13.11	15.64	14.12	42.87
Fruit	8.08	9.14	7.49	24.71
Cereals	8.10	8.80	7.45	24.35
Cheese	9.60	10.09	8.83	28.52
Biscuits	6.50	6.12	6.79	19.41
Confectionery	5.45	5.99	6.35	17.79
Soft drinks	8.50	8.23	9.98	26.71
Alcohol	12.20	10.39	14.24	36.83
Pet food	4.50	5.30	4.25	14.05
Sub total	**94.72**	**98.93**	**99.64**	**293.29**
Other Household Expenses				
Body care	7.40	7.98	8.34	23.72
Cleaning	7.90	5.32	5.98	19.20
Clothing/shoes	72.09	17.07	32.08	121.24
Hairdressing	15.50	—	8.00	23.50
Medical	—	35.00	—	35.00
Legal	—	—	200.00	200.00
Veterinary	—	14.89	—	14.89
Sub total	**102.89**	**80.26**	**254.40**	**437.55**
Transport				
Fares	24.00	28.50	22.50	75.00
Petrol	38.00	32.50	40.00	110.50

Table 7: Example of a Spending Record (cont)

	January £	February £	March £	Total £
Transport (cont)				
Oil	—	5.99	—	5.99
Repair/service	125.30	—	—	125.30
Car Cleaning	3.50	—	3.50	7.00
Sub total	**190.80**	**66.99**	**66.00**	**323.79**
Entertainment				
Pub	47.50	32.90	24.36	104.76
Cinema/Video	7.40	5.00	12.00	24.40
Restaurant	24.50	—	27.63	52.13
Clubs	—	100.00	—	100.00
Sports equipment	—	35.00	4.75	39.75
Cards and gifts	9.99	—	30.00	39.99
Baby-sitting	18.00	12.00	14.00	44.00
Periodicals	12.30	10.50	11.35	34.15
Books	—	5.00	7.49	12.49
Holidays	—	—	135.75	135.75
Sub total	**119.69**	**200.40**	**267.33**	**587.42**
Grand Total	**1,348.85**	**1,066.15**	**1,220.61**	**3,635.61**

This record does not include debt repayment or savings. These contributions can be included if you wish, or listed separately. There are also categories not included here which might be applicable to your own situation, such as the cost of cigarettes, and so on. Each record has to be compiled *by* the individual *for* the individual. It will tell you things about yourself that may come as a surprise. We are what we consume!

The exercise of recording your pattern of spending means that you will begin to identify where savings can be made. Many of these savings will have added health benefits: eating less meat and more vegetables, cycling to work rather than taking the bus, cutting down on alcohol, giving up cigarettes and so on will increase your all-round fitness and vitality.

Yet again, it can be seen that an apparent problem (having to cut down on spending) is in fact a disguised opportunity to be healthier.

Add to this the fact that the more healthy you get, the more positive will be your frame of mind, and you will be entering a virtuous circle of recovery, rather than a vicious circle of debt. In other words, the more you try to improve your life, the more beneficial influences there will be to help you.

The spending record is an incredibly simple but amazingly useful device. It tells you exactly where your money goes. I derived it from a system of record keeping for a small business, where everything has to be accounted for, and where categorization of spending is standard accounting practice. Only later did I realize that such an approach would work wonders for planning my personal spending. Later still, I discovered that the spending record is recommended to candidates of Debtors Anonymous in the US. The Debtors Anonymous organization considers it absolutely essential to any programme of debt reduction. I can endorse their opinion wholeheartedly, and so will you. So start right now to record your spending.

Points to Remember

- You will find it difficult to construct a spending plan without first recording your spending.
- Record every expenditure you make, preferably at the time but at least at the end of each day.
- Divide your spending up into categories and record these weekly or monthly.
- Begin to identify where economies can be made.
- Recognize that the process of making economies will be beneficial to your health and self-image.

STEP 6

Plan Your Spending

By now you will have made a firm commitment to get out of debt, and you should have begun to keep a daily record of your spending. The next step is to decide on a spending plan. This does not have to be particularly elaborate, but it does require some careful thought. Before constructing your personal spending plan (which you may prefer to call a budget), there are a few things to bear in mind.

First of all, you are *not* going to construct a plan which gives as much as possible to the people to whom you owe money—your creditors, leaving you with only the bare minimum to exist on. Such a plan will almost certainly fail. Everybody needs little luxuries and treats to look forward to, otherwise life wouldn't be worth living.

In constructing a spending plan, you must decide what you can do without, or with much less of, but you cannot leave out what you feel you must do to enjoy life, whether it is going out to the pub a couple of times a week, or attending the social club, or following your favourite sport.

The second thing to remember when constructing your spending plan is that while you are determined to pay off your creditors, you will not live your life for them. If you are deeply in debt, it is probable that there will not be enough money left to meet the minimum requirements of all your creditors. Don't worry about that for now. The rule is that you will first of all ensure that your commitments to secured creditors are met; after which you will treat all your unsecured creditors equally. Techniques for dealing with creditors are discussed fully in Step 7.

You will have identified from your spending record those items which are essential expenditure. These will include mortgage payments or rent, utilities (heating and lighting) bills, food, some household goods, some clothing, essential travel (such as fares to work), and possibly court-ordered payments such as fines and maintenance. Although all of these categories come under the title of essential expenditure, this does not mean to say that savings cannot be made in several areas.

Mortgages

Two-thirds of householders in this country live in a mortgaged home. For most people, the largest item of essential expenditure in their monthly budget will be mortgage payments. For people in debt to other lenders as well, the mortgage will take priority for repayment. This is because a mortgage is secured on your home, and if you default you can easily lose it.

Unfortunately, the incidence of default on mortgages is rising, and with it comes a rapid increase in the number of people made homeless through repossessions. For this reason, it is essential that you tackle any debt problems long before you run the risk of defaulting on your mortgage.

. No one wants to lose the roof over their head. Equally, you would not want to lose all the money you have already repaid to the mortgage lender. So it is essential that you understand exactly the various types of mortgage options available and what risks they imply.

Repayment or Endowment?

Traditionally, most mortgages taken out by people in the 1960s and 1970s, were of the repayment type. Under these schemes you repaid all of the principal of the loan, plus the interest, usually over a 25 year period. At the end of the term you would own your house outright, but have no extra cash.

Endowment mortgages, on the other hand, have been heavily promoted during the last few years, to the extent that two out of three new mortgages taken out are of the endowment type. These promise the possibility of paying off your mortgage over the term (again, usually 25 years but sometimes longer) while giving you a lump sum of cash at the end of the period. This happy state of affairs is achieved by having the company providing the mortgage invest on your behalf. You pay interest on the money borrowed plus a premium for investment. You will also have to insure yourself against possible non-payment. All of these charges usually add up to a heftier monthly payment than with the repayment option. But then there is always the promise of a few thousand pounds spare cash for your old age.

Endowment mortgages would appear to give you the best of both worlds, but beware! The performance of the fund in which you are investing is only as good as that of the managers who run it. It is an established fact that the majority of fund managers perform worse than the market averages.

This also means that when the stock-market falls, the value of your accumulated investment is likely to fall with it. During the great crash of October 1987, most funds were heavily invested in the stock market, and managed to shrink the value of their holdings. You might argue that over the long haul this doesn't matter, as losses will be balanced by gains in the future. This may well be true, but the chances are that you could be at least as well off starting your own personal investment programme, as discussed in Step 10.

There are other drawbacks with endowment mortgages. Because of the relatively poor investment performance of many of the funds in which you are investing, allied to the fees paid to intermediaries from your early instalments, if you redeem the mortgage in the early years, you will get much less than the value of your contributions. There may also be penalties levied by the lender for doing so, amounting to as much as three months' interest payments. This is less likely for repayment mortgages, although you should always check beforehand. It is much better, if you have an endowment mortgage and wish to change its terms, to do so within the framework of your existing loan. However, you will probably be charged an arrangement fee for any changes made.

If you have a repayment mortgage, it may be advantageous for you to consider switching to one with a cheaper rate, even with the administration costs involved. With the current climate of fierce competition there is quite a diversity of interest rates and mortgage terms available. It is a relatively simple matter to work out the best deals. You may in the first instance contact a mortgage broker and discuss your requirements. Mortgage brokers advertise in the financial pages of the popular press, and are listed in telephone directories. Like insurance brokers, they should be able to find you the best package to suit your needs. However, mortgage brokers often deal only in endowment mortgages. If they do arrange a repayment mortgage, they are likely to ask for a fee of around 1 per cent of the total cost of the loan.

If you want to stick to a repayment mortgage, then probably the best action to take is to ring or write to all the small and large building societies to find out what terms they can offer. A list can be obtained from the Building Societies Association (see Appendix 1 for this address).

A number of specialist journals, such as *Mortgage Magazine*, are also available to guide you through the mortgage maze. They often have helpful tables summarizing the costs of borrowing at different interest rates, or from different lenders. It is well worth purchasing one of these magazines to help you consider the various options.

If you are finding it difficult to meet your existing mortgage repayments, you will probably want to reduce your monthly payments. There are several ways in which you can do this. One is to increase the repayment period, thereby reducing the monthly outgoings. Another is to switch to a lower fixed-interest rate. Or you might be tempted to take out a foreign currency mortgage, a pension mortgage, or an equity-linked scheme. These options are considered below.

Extending the Term of Repayment

In principle, if you are in financial difficulties and want to extend your mortgage (of whatever type) to reduce the payments, then this may well be worth considering. This would be especially relevant if you have paid off a number of years of the mortgage already. However, remember that you are continuing to pay extra interest for the extended time of the mortgage, and that this is not generally a good idea if it can be avoided.

Another possibility is to ask your lender whether it is acceptable for you to make interest-only payments for a while until your finances are under better control. Lenders will often agree to this for relatively short periods, of six months or so,for example, although they will eventually want to see payments being made to reduce the principal of the loan.

One of the types of mortgage currently on offer which should be avoided is that which charges a lower interest rate than that currently charged and adds the unpaid extra interest to your mortgage at some future date. The mortgage brokers quaintly call this 'rolling up' the unpaid interest. What it in fact means is that you are paying interest on the interest, and you are already aware of the devastating effects of compound interest. This is a very expensive and painful way of postponing current pain for future debt agony. A national newspaper calculated recently that up to 75 per cent of a person's after-tax income could be eventually swallowed up by deferred interest schemes. The situation would be even worse if in the future your income were to fall through illness or unemployment.

In general, it is better to bite the bullet and arrange to repay your mortgage at current interest rates, even if you do have to extend the term of repayment or pay interest-only for a short period of time. At least you will know that you will one day be rid of the debt, instead of adding to it in the future.

What about Fixing the Mortgage Rate?

Some financiers are spotting the potential for getting more customers by offering schemes whereby the rates are fixed for a given period— usually around three years. When interest rates move up fast over a short period, this often seems an attractive option.

It should be remembered, however, that interest rates are extremely volatile, and can go down as well as up. A lot depends upon your view of the future for the world economy. I expect there to be a secular decline in economic activity during the early to mid-1990s, leading to a recession, or even a depression. If this is so, then deflation would take hold, which would mean falling prices. (See Step 10 for a full explanation of this logic.) This in turn would cause interest rates to fall as debt is liquidated and the Chancellor attempts to inject more demand into the economy. If that happens, anyone taking out a mortgage at this or any similar time would be hog-tied on a fixed-interest scheme. If, on the other hand, I'm wrong and raging inflation returns, then interest rates will shoot up and you will be on to a winner.

Should You Take Out a Foreign Currency Mortgage?

A growing number of companies have been offering foreign currency mortgages. These may at first appear very attractive, offering exceptionally low-interest rates compared to the current high levels in the UK. However, you should consider very carefully the possible costs and consequences of switching to a foreign currency mortgage.

The sterling exchange rate is very vulnerable to difficult times. High domestic interest rates are no guarantee that there will not be a run on the pound. For example, in February 1988 the Australian dollar dropped 6 per cent within a fortnight in response to international fears of its uncompetitiveness. This happened despite Australia's high domestic interest rates. Any similar run on the pound sterling would radically increase the price of your foreign currency mortgage. You might be repaying, 10 per cent more pounds than last month because the pound had depreciated by that much against the Swiss Franc. So instead of paying £500, you are now paying £550—and there is no guarantee that the sterling slide, once begun, would not continue.

Exchange rate changes have become extremely volatile in recent years. Consider the pound/dollar exchange rate, which fell to a low point of $1.10 / £1 in early 1986, before shooting up to $1.80 to the pound 18 months later. This represented a 63 per cent depreciation of the dollar against the pound. A similar change in the opposite direction could represent another nasty swing for those people who have taken out a foreign currency mortgage in dollars. The pound has been in decline against the dollar ever since the American Civil War, when it was worth $16. Upward momentum of the pound against the dollar has not persisted for very long during this great bear market, characterized as it is by a falling pound.

I have used the dollar as an example, but the same is true of other foreign currencies. If you are still keen on the idea of a foreign currency mortgage, then let me suggest that you take one out in ECUs. The ECU is an artificial currency used within the Common Market—the initials stand for European Currency Unit.

The ECU rate is calculated from a 'basket' of currencies used within the EEC, and as such it is less volatile than any individual currency against the pound. The ECU/£ exchange rate is likely to become even less volatile now that sterling has joined the European Monetary System (EMS) and is allowed to fluctuate only within designated parameters, before being supported by EEC central banks.

If you take out an ECU foreign currency mortgage, then the chances are that you will pay a higher rate of interest for it than for other foreign currencies (although not as high as present UK rates), but you are more likely to be protected from rapid swings in currency exchange rates, which would immediately affect your mortgage repayments. You may also take out additional insurance to hedge against currency swings, but this will add to the cost of the mortgage.

Pension Mortgages

Again, pension mortgages have been touted by financial advisers as wonderfully tax-efficient, since you receive tax relief both on your interest payments on the first £30,000 of the mortgage and on your contributions to a pension scheme. The capital part of the mortgage is secured on your pension, and is repaid out of a lump sum paid to you on retirement. Meanwhile, you pay interest only.

If you need to pay the lowest possible amount to the lender, then it may be worth considering this type of mortgage or re-mortgage. However, remember that if you are relatively young, you might be entering into a very long-term scheme, meaning you will pay a great deal of interest to the lender. Consider also that the intermediary will be looking for his or her usual commissions.

In general, I would not recommend a pension mortgage. It is yet another device for ensuring that a sizeable proportion of your income goes into the hands of the moneylender throughout your working life. If you can you should plan to repay your mortgage as quickly as possible, to avoid paying too much interest.

Equity-linked Mortgages

These are a relatively new introduction in this country, again touted for the so-called tax advantages. Investments in a Personal Equity Plan (PEP), introduced by the government as an incentive to wider share ownership, are allowed to grow tax free up to a certain threshold. Fully 75 per cent of a PEP must be invested directly in UK equities or in Unit Trusts holding UK shares.

Under an equity-linked mortgage, you pay a sum of money monthly into a PEP which is managed on your behalf. You will be charged an annual fee for this service. The growth in value of the PEP over the period of the mortgage is supposed to repay the sum borrowed, while you pay interest monthly, collecting tax relief in the normal way.

Unfortunately, investment in equities is quite high risk, even in blue-chip companies. Recent experience has shown that UK stocks are not immune from major crashes. A long-term decline could result in your owing the lender quite a bit of money in relation to your depleted PEP.

Equity-linked mortgages are, in my opinion, high risk, especially today. You shouldn't allow the vagaries of investor sentiment on the stock-market to affect the security of your home. Avoid PEP mortgages for the sake of your financial and emotional health.

Renting

What about the other third of us (me included) who rent a place to live? You may feel a bit sick about having missed out on the 1980s property boom. If so, I've got good news for you. Private sector rents are likely to fall over the next few years as the supply of letting properties increases. So you should get more choice, lower rents, and still be able to save for the time when you feel that you can afford to buy a home.

In all housing matters, there is a degree of inertia when it comes to thinking of a move. Changing your habitat is a distressing experience, even for the most well-adjusted of us. I am from an Air Force background, where the family moved frequently, so subconsciously

I feel that I ought to move every few years. On the other hand, my wife is a real homebody, and hates being uprooted.

If you are already renting and want to cut down your monthly or weekly payments, you can try to renegotiate them. One way of doing this is simply to ask the landlord for a reduction when the lease expires. He or she might agree; since reletting will cause extra hassle and expense. Another method is to go to the local authority rent tribunal—but beware, this can backfire—in at least one case I know of the rent was raised! Another way of tackling the problem, especially if you are self-employed, is to form a limited company and offer your landlord a company let. It is not difficult to form a limited company, it takes about a month if you do it through a specialist firm (they advertise in the national quality press and in *Exchange and Mart*), and costs about £70. You can then offer your landlord a greater degree of security, in exchange for a lower rent and/or a longer lease. Alternatively, you could upgrade your accommodation by offering a company let on a three or four-bedroomed house and subletting to sharers. You might even get yourself a free room if you charge enough to the sharers.

However, nowadays it is not usually necessary to be able to offer a company let to get a good rental deal. The recent legislation introducing shorthold tenancies allows for rental periods of up to a year with no risk to the private landlord. This legislation has done a lot to improve the supply of housing for renters recently, which again puts downward pressure on rents.

Poll Tax

The poll tax, or 'community charge', as the Government prefers to call it, has come as a heavy blow to many people who are on low incomes, or who are heavily in debt.

Some opposition groups have called for non-payment, arguing that if enough people refuse to pay, then the courts will become clogged with cases and the system will be unworkable. While this may be true, non-payment will also result in your being summonsed. If a liability order is approved by the court, your employers may be asked to deduct money from your wages or salary to pay the charge. Alternatively, you may also face a fine; and, depending on what action your local council decides to take, bailiffs may descend on your home to seize goods which will be sold to raise money to pay off the debt.

If you are on a low income with little in the way of savings, then you may be entitled to a rebate of up to 80 per cent of the poll tax. If you haven't done so already, you should contact your local social security office for an application form without delay.

Utilities

You may think it is difficult to save in this area, but economies can be made. If you live in a centrally heated home, turn the thermostat down! You don't really need to bask in 70° heat all day. Wear a pullover more often and save on heating bills.

It may help to consider opening a budget account with your local gas and electricity boards. By paying a fixed amount each month to the utility company, you avoid being confronted with large quarterly bills. Also, if you are already in arrears with the gas and electricity boards, it is possible to arrange for these outstanding sums to be paid off gradually over a period of time with your monthly budget contribution.

The gas and electricity suppliers are very familiar with customers falling behind with payments, and will only cut you off if you fail to communicate with them and explain your difficulties. So don't wait for them to disconnect you before dealing with them. If you are in this situation be sure to read the step 7, which offers advice on dealing with creditors.

Food and Other Household Essentials

Obviously, you will want to budget very carefully for food. One easy way to save money is to buy in bulk one day a week from your local supermarket or discount store. That way you avoid frequent and expensive trips down to the corner shop for high-priced food. Of course, it is usually cheaper to add a trip to the market for fruit and vegetables. Other household essentials, such as cleaning materials, light bulbs, cookware and so on can also be picked up very cheaply at open-air markets and even at car-boot sales. Budget carefully and shop around, and considerable monthly savings can be made.

Clothes

A remarkable phenomenon is beginning to occur in the high street. The downturn in consumer spending, brought about by high interest rates and saturated levels of personal debt, is causing a reversal of the 1980s retailing boom. Retailers are starting to feel the pinch, and are trying to boost sales and to cut costs.

As they do so, deflation is beginning to take hold in the clothing industry. Prices are tumbling as shop proprietors unload unsold stocks. In the smaller shops, you can even bargain over the sale prices, although it is not so easy in Marks and Spencer. Don't be afraid to ask—they can only say no!

In general, and especially if clothing sprees are one of your bad debt habits, it is better to buy better quality clothes, less often. Good quality clothing may be more expensive, but lasts longer and doesn't go out of style so quickly. Wear 'classic' clothes and they will feel good, look good, and not leave you feeling unfashionable.

Of course, if you are really economizing, there are always the great standbys—the charity second-hand shops and the discount retail chains. There is nothing wrong with these, you can pick up some real bargains if you enjoy browsing. Jumble sales are a good bet also—but get there early!

Essential Travel

Most of us have to travel quite far to work, and in addition may have to pay other essential travel expenses, such as bus fares to get children to school. If it is at all practical, then you should find cheaper means of transport. For example, if it is feasible it will be cheaper in the long run to buy a second-hand bicycle to travel to work than to keep paying bus fares. Similarly, annual season tickets are a cheap way of getting to work for the long-distance rail traveller. You may find that switching from rail to coach travel, or from commuting in your own car to car-sharing offer substantial savings on your journey to and from work.

Some employers already give interest-free season ticket loans to staff so that they can take advantage of the cheapest annual rate. The money is usually deducted direct from wages or salary on a monthly basis. If your employer offers such a scheme, then by all means take advantage of it. If your employer does not, why not ask if it can be introduced?

Court-ordered Expenditure

Unless your circumstances have changed dramatically, such as through the loss of a job, then you are unlikely to be able to reduce these expenses. If you have experienced an unavoidable and drastic fall in income, then you can apply to the court for a reduction or rescheduling of payments. However, the chances of success are limited unless it can be argued that you really are in desperate straits.

It is important that you do not default on court-ordered payments. Distress warrants could be awarded against you for the seizure of goods, or you could even end up in prison for non-payment.

Discretionary Expenditure

Your list of categories of essential expenditure need not be very long. It should include only those items which are absolutely essential for your basic existence. A large number of items which many people have come to believe are essential are not really so. Examples are cars and telephones. Only people who work from home must have the latter.

In preparing your list of discretionary spending items you must identify areas where savings can be made. Some can be done away with altogether until your circumstances improve. The object of this exercise is to trim off the flab, so that reasonable provision can be made for your unsecured creditors.

Pensions and Life Assurance

If you are in an employer's pension scheme, then it is likely that you will place this category of spending in the essentials list. Nevertheless, many schemes, especially personal pensions, allow you to reduce or suspend monthly payments without penalty. If money is really tight, you may wish to consider this course of action. However, in general it is wise to maintain your pension payments, even at a reduced level.

The same goes for life assurance. People with dependents are going to want and need life assurance, but it may be advantageous to stick to the simple term assurance, where your dependents are assured of a lump sum if you die or are severely injured. If you are already in a scheme where part of the contributions go towards an endowment savings plan, you may wish to consider releasing the savings to pay off some debts. However, this is only likely to be a viable option if the plan has been in force for a number of years. Endowment plans show poor returns if they are cashed in too early.

Motoring Expenses

In the affluent 1980s, a car became much more than a means of transport. It became a badge of rank. If you were not, by the time you were thirty, driving a car with alloy wheels and a sunroof, made by a well-known German manufacturer, then you might well have considered yourself a failure.

Happily, this attitude is already on the way out. This has happened in part as a result of the pendulum of popular opinion swinging away from such naked displays of affluence, and partly as a consequence of our greater concern for the environment. Cars are beginning to be seen as strictly utilitarian vehicles, for getting people from A to B in maximum safety and with minimum pollution.

The first thing you need to consider, therefore, especially if you are seriously in debt, is whether or not you can survive without a car. Do you own it out of vanity or necessity? Unless you live in a remote rural area, you can probably get around by using public transport, or better still a bicycle. It will no doubt remain fashionable to be fit and slim, and cycling to and from work is one good way of achieving this goal. You can sell your car, buy a good second-hand bike or a cheap new one from a large discount store, and use the proceeds from the sale of the car to pay off some of your most urgent debts—especially credit card debts.

If you do live in a rural area, or literally can't stand the thought of life without a car, then you should consider trading down. You can get a cheap, fairly reliable and easy-to-fix model through the local paper or at a car auction. If you are afraid of buying a lemon, and don't know much about cars, take a knowledgeable friend along.

You can cut down on car maintenance bills by doing as much of the work as you can yourself, perhaps attending a maintenance class in order to gain the knowledge to do so. If you do need to use a garage for major repairs, then you must shop around, and get several firm quotes for the work before proceeding.

If you decide to live without a car, and have to resort to public transport, it's not a bad way to travel if you plan your journeys right, especially by taking advantage of off-peak rates. Taking the occasional taxi for a night out is also going to be a lot cheaper than the upkeep of a car. So think about it, which do you prefer: being heavily in debt and driving a smart car, or living within your means and laying firm financial foundations for the future? You can always treat yourself to a car when you can genuinely afford it.

Telephone Expenses

Again, the telephone has come to be considered a necessity, but is this in fact true? If you use the telephone mainly for chatting to your friends and relations, then you could simply switch to the old-fashioned art of letter writing. If you still need to enjoy conversation, then budget for a phone card, which will at least avoid the temptation to carry on at length and run up a large phone bill.

If you must have a telephone, then consider switching to a company other than British Telecom for your long-distance calls. For a small annual fee you can usually enjoy up to 20 per cent off long-distance and international calls, and also receive itemized billing. Alternatively, you could consider installing a British Telecom payphone. However, the quarterly rental for this will be higher, so it is better to be disciplined in the use of your ordinary phone. This includes a firm rule to make non-essential business calls only after 1 p.m.; and personal calls after 6 p.m.

Dining Out

If there is one sure way to get into debt fast, it is through dining out a lot and paying with credit cards. When I look back through my old spending records, at least a quarter of overspending was incurred in restaurants.

If you have destroyed your cards and started to plan your expenditure, then the chances are that you will still want to treat yourself to the occasional meal out, but that you will be a lot more careful about choosing the restaurant. You will also benefit from taking cash, so that you can stay within your budget. Restaurateurs will tell you that customers definitely spend more when they use a credit card than with cash, and that they are more likely to leave a large tip.

Better still, you will probably begin to develop a taste for eating in more often. If you wish to remain sociable, then start giving more dinner parties. You don't have to go mad and give all your guests steak—try cheaper vegetarian meals which are better for you and will be enjoyed just as much. If your friends want to reciprocate, they can choose to do so at an expensive restaurant or at home—it's their affair.

For the avid diner there are also numerous guides to cheaper eating places. Avoiding pretentious places can mean concentrating on good food, and not paying a premium for it. One of the most delectable and best value fish restaurants in England looks on the inside like a truck stop. This doesn't stop gourmets driving long distances to eat there.

As for sending out for a pizza or other kinds of take-away food, making a little extra effort and creating your own is a lot cheaper, good fun and you can add all your favourite toppings at little extra cost. So tear up those delivery service phone numbers!

Alcohol and Tobacco

It is very easy in our culture to spend an awful lot of money on alcoholic drink. Many people seem to believe that they should imbibe lots of alcohol as a means of enjoying themselves. This attitude is constantly reinforced by advertising, as well as by the socializing we do. Tobacco is becoming less socially acceptable, although many people who would otherwise consider themselves non-smokers find themselves smoking at social gatherings.

The short answer to the problem of spending too much on alcohol is to decide when or how often you will treat yourself to a visit to the pub or wine bar, and how much you will spend. Take along only that particular amount of money. You will gradually reduce your consumption over time as you find that you need less and less.

If you are as yet unable to contemplate giving up cigarettes entirely, consumption can be reduced if you decide in advance when you will smoke, and give yourself a daily ration. That way you could have a smoke during breaks or after meals, but could avoid smoking while actually working. You will gain both health and financial benefits.

One situation to beware of is the after-hours drinking session with your workmates, when you all go straight down the pub. This can lead to rapid loss of inhibitions, large rounds being bought, lots of cigarettes being smoked—in short havoc being played with your spending plan. Make an excuse and avoid such sessions altogether, or at the very least make an excuse and leave early.

Newspapers, Magazines and Books

The costs of taking a daily newspaper, plus perhaps an evening one as well as a couple of magazines a week can soon add up, especially if you get them delivered. By now, if you have filled in your annual expenditure sheet, you will already have realized this. My total was £300 annually for a morning paper, an evening paper and a weekly magazine, which rose to over £600 when I included regular book purchases. Quite a sum!

There are obviously substantial savings to be made from cutting down on your purchases of reading material. If you are like me, and can't pass a bookshop without browsing and being tempted to buy, then one of the best deterrents is to leave your credit card at home, if you haven't already cut it up.

If you are not already a member, join a public library. It will save the avid bookbuyer a fortune, unless you are consistently late in returning the books. Remember, you can also borrow a wide selection of records, so the music enthusiast should also take heed.

As for newspapers, do you really read them every day? Perhaps you should restrict yourself to buying only on those days when you know that you will have time to read. If you have the papers delivered—cancel them—why pay a premium because you can't be bothered to walk to the newsagents? Again, you can drop by your local library to catch up on the week's news if you absolutely have to be informed. You should be able to halve your reading bill by practising a degree of self-restraint.

TV and Video

The TV, and latterly the video recorder, are excellent inventions for people who are planning to get out of debt. Instead of going out to the cinema and spending lots of money on tickets, you can rent a film for a fraction of the price. So if you own a video, great, keep it unless you really don't use it much and would rather sell it to reduce your debt burden.

On the other hand, if you are renting a TV and video, you are probably making a big mistake. Just add up the annual rental costs and set these against the costs of buying second-hand machines. You may well find that nine months to a year's rental expenditure will buy a good second-hand machine which would last two to three years. You may even be able to buy a cheap new machine on interest-free credit.

So think about saving the rental and buying a TV or video instead. There will be lots of bargains in your local newspaper. You could even send back the rented TV and video, save the rental fee for a few months, and then buy the items you need.

Going Out

You should still allow a certain amount of money in your spending plan for trips to the cinema, theatre, exhibitions, shows etc. The trick here is to decide what you can afford to spend, and plan your treats in advance.

Planning in advance does not mean that you can't take advantage of special last-minute stand-by deals. These are ideal for people on a budget. Remember also that if you are a student or in a younger age group, you can often take advantage of further discounts. You will need a concessionary card to do this, so it is again worth making the small investment to obtain one in order to save money in the future.

Sports and Hobbies

You may be reluctant to cut down in this area, especially if you are passionate about your favourite sport or other kind of pastime. If it's not too expensive, then there is no problem. However, if it is an expensive hobby, then you may find that you will have to cut down for a while, or even drop it until things improve. I enjoy windsurfing, but I had virtually to give up the sport for a year or so until things improved financially.

If you have expensive equipment, it may be worth selling it until you can afford to start again. Take up a cheaper pastime instead, or do more of the other games and hobbies you enjoy.

Sports club membership may also be a hangover from your high-spending days. Ask yourself if you really use the club that much. If you don't, you could save yourself a packet by opting out. Try running round the block instead, or go to your local public sports hall.

Presents

You will probably want to buy presents at certain times of the year. However, these can be budgeted for, and do not have to be expensive. It is understandable that you will want to give presents to children, but your love for them is not measured by the amount you spend. Adults will understand if you decide not to give presents, but instead send a card or an affectionate letter.

Remember the effect of extra spending at Christmas in your spending plan. You may wish to put aside some of the savings you've made in other areas of discretionary spending to ensure that you have an enjoyable festive season. Again, the trick is to plan ahead.

Holidays

You should have holidays—everybody needs a break. My own preference is for a few days off several times a year, rather than a big splurge once a year. One way to save money on holidays is to consider the more active variety—such as a cycling and camping trip. Foreign holidays should be avoided, unless you are being offered an exceptionally cheap deal. Block bookings are a good idea, where you negotiate a substantial discount or even a free trip in return for putting a large party together.

Another cheap way to travel is as a courier for one of the international companies. A friend of mine flies regularly across the Atlantic for a nominal fee in return for transporting documents. On one occasion she even got to fly on Concorde for next to nothing!

Allocating Money for Debt Repayment

As a precursor to your plan to get out of debt, you will have added up the total of your unsecured debts—racking your brains to think of people or institutions to whom you owe money. The final figure may be more or less than you thought you owed, but at least you will know what it is.

Once you have worked out the total debt, you must identify what proportion of it you owe to each creditor. For example, if your total debt is £10,000 and you owe £1500 to Barclaycard, then 15 per cent of the total is owed to that particular creditor.

Any amount should be dealt with as shown in Table 8:

Table 8

$$\text{Percentage owed} = \frac{\text{debt}}{\text{total}} \times 100$$

in our example $\dfrac{1{,}500}{10{,}000} \times 100 = 15\%$

The calculation is not difficult, just divide the smaller number by the larger, and multiply by 100 to get the percentage. Use a calculator—it makes the sums much easier. Once you have worked out the percentage owed to each creditor, to calculate how much each should be repaid monthly, you simply multiply the percentage owed to each creditor by the amount you have identified in your spending plan as being available to repay all your unsecured creditors.

For example, suppose you have £200 available each month to repay creditors , and you have ten of them. Each will get an amount proportionate to their share of total debt, as shown in Table 9:

Table 9

Creditor	Share of total	Monthly repayment
Barclaycard	7.5%	£15
Access	12%	£24

Creditor	Share of total	Monthly repayment
Storecard 1	12.5%	£25
Storecard 2	18%	£36
Bank loan 1	10%	£20
Bank loan 2	9.5%	£19
Finance house	11%	£22
Finance house	5.5%	£11
Father	8%	· £16
Sister	6%	£12
Total	100%	£200

If the total owed falls below that demanded monthly by some or all of your creditors—don't worry. You are going to negotiate with them, one by one. Techniques for doing this are explained in the next chapter.

Stay Out of Debt One Day at a Time

So far, you will have resolved to record your spending, analyse your spending habits, and plan your future spending. Congratulations— you are now firmly on the road to a life free from debt.

In order to achieve your goal quickly and resolutely, it is important that you do not slip back into the debt habit. *Do* leave home without your credit cards, and try leaving your cheque book and bank cash card behind as well. Withdraw from the bank only the sum of money you require daily or weekly as indicated by your spending plan.

The best way to approach your new financial life is to resolve, just for today, that you will not borrow for any purpose whatsoever.

Once you have decided not to go into debt just for today, you will begin to find creative ways around the fact that you don't have very much money. You may find that there are sources of available cash which you have forgotten about, such as money due to you from other sources which you have not bothered to chase up. You will find that it is not so difficult to forgo a visit to the pub or the cinema just for one day, or to turn down that invitation for an expensive meal.

Tomorrow, you will again resolve not to go into debt for the whole day. It doesn't seem so long, one day at a time. In fact, every morning thereafter when you get up you can resolve not to go into debt for another day. Before you know it, you will have unlearned the debt habit.

It seems terribly simple—after all, everybody can go a day without getting into debt, can't they? In fact, it is no more difficult than changing any other damaging habit. This method works for giving up smoking, for example. The subconscious mind has quite a lot of difficulty with the concept of giving up bad habits 'forever', so it is much easier to grasp the idea of giving up one day at a time.

As you repeat your daily resolve not to get into debt, you will become ever more creative in finding ways of economizing without necessarily compromising your quality of living. To take but one example, you may find that cheaper food is not necessarily boring, and is almost certainly better for you than more expensive fare. You may also find that you are able to live with less and less in the way of material toys and gadgets; and that you increasingly appreciate the simple pleasures of life.

Learning not to go into debt one day at a time will begin to restore your self-respect, and repair your self-image. You will be taking positive steps along the road to prosperity. So start today, or at least resolve to begin first thing tomorrow morning. Don't get into debt—one day at a time.

Points to Remember

- Getting out of debt means planning your spending. You will be able to use your spending record to construct a spending plan.

- You must decide carefully what is essential spending. Only then can you trim back on discretionary spending. There are bound to be many areas in which you can save without sacrificing your life-style too much.

- Planning your spending does not mean that you give everything to your creditors and little or nothing to yourself. Decide what you can sensibly afford to repay to your creditors.

- Treat all unsecured creditors on the same basis. Plan to pay each in proportion to their share of your total debt.

- Stick to your spending plan. Resolve to stay out of debt one day at a time.

STEP 7

Negotiate with Your Creditors

You are not going to get rid of your debt problem by running away from your creditors! It is dangerous to keep ignoring them. The problem won't go away, and you will risk being taken to court, with all the stress and worry that entails. The only way you are going to avoid this kind of stress is to negotiate with your creditors—communicate with them!

It is quite likely that a large proportion of your outstanding debt is made up of credit card debt and/or bank loans. The point to remember here is that the institutions which grant these loans *expect* a proportion of their customers to default. That is why the interest rates are so high—remember that the higher the risk of lending money, the higher is the interest-rate demanded by the lenders. Credit card interest charges are high because almost anyone is allowed to borrow, making the risk of default high.

The big banks and finance houses are accustomed to having to chase their bad debts with nasty letters or legal action. They also realize that if the debt is unsecured, then they are likely to reclaim only a fraction of the total if you are sued or bankrupted. Secured creditors will enjoy priority. If, on the other hand, they can arrange repayment with you even at a reduced level of contributions, they will eventually be able to claw back all or most of the debt.

If you make a clean breast of your problems, creditors, whether secured or unsecured, are much more likely to deal fairly and leniently with you. The institutions dealing with the debt are large, and may appear faceless, but they are made up of people just like you! Get on friendly terms with those people, and you will be able to negotiate a good deal for both parties.

Mortgage Arrears

In recent years, mortgage arrears have risen sharply as hundreds of thousands of people have faced increased payments, reduced incomes, or both. As with other kinds of debt, it is important for you to realize that you are not alone.

The scale of this problem is such that the Council of Mortgage Lenders has published a set of guidelines (available from the Building Societies Association - see Appendix 1 for their address), which it expects its members, and other respectable lending institutions, to abide by. In any case, lenders prefer not to repossess property, which they might then have to sell at a price lower than the outstanding mortgage in a depressed market. If they can possibly help you to keep a roof over your head, they will.

To quote from the guidelines, which are entitled 'Handling of Mortgage Arrears':

When a borrower falls into arrears through no fault of his or her own, the problem is handled both sympathetically and positively. This requires that the borrower co-operates with the lender, in particular by reacting to correspondence.

The key point in dealing successfully with arrears problems is that the borrower should make contact with the lender (or vice versa) at the earliest possible time. The borrower is likely to anticipate problems before the lender becomes aware of them. Lenders want borrowers to contact them before arrears begin to build up.

There you have it from the horse's mouth! Lenders are not ogres, they will help you in any way they can. This code of practice goes on to say that it is very definitely up to the lender to ensure that the borrower is a good risk, with the implication being that some lenders are themselves partly to blame for allowing people in vulnerable positions to take up large loans.

Mortgage arrears are generally handled in the following manner. When one or two payments have been missed, the lender will write to the borrower. If there is no response to the letter, then the lender will attempt to achieve direct contact, usually by telephoning and attempting to arrange a meeting.

It is only if payments continue to be missed and no meeting can be arranged that legal proceedings are likely to be undertaken to foreclose on the property.

So the golden rule in dealing with creditors, and in particular with secured creditors is *communicate!* Don't be an ostrich and bury your head in the sand, hoping your problems will disappear. Be brave, pick up the phone and do it now!

Solving the Mortgage Arrears Problem

The guidelines for mortgage lenders suggest various ways for lenders to assist borrowers in dealing with arrears, although it is noted that 'each case has to be dealt with on its individual merits within a very broad framework'.

The option of increasing the term of repayment is mentioned, although it is noted that if the mortgage is large and the extension period not very long, this may not make a significant difference to the amount of the monthly repayments.

It is suggested that an endowment mortgage may be switched to a repayment mortgage in order to reduce the monthly contributions. However, as mentioned in Step 6, you should be wary of losing out if your policy has not yet accumulated a value commensurate with the contributions you have already made to it. But bear in mind that you could use the cash value of the endowment mortgage, sold through a broker, to realize its maximum potential, and use the money made to pay off mortgage arrears or other debt. You could then take out a new repayment mortgage over 25 years.

The option of deferring interest is considered, but it is noted that this option is realistic only for short periods. For example, if you are temporarily out of a job but are confident of your prospects of getting another without much delay; or if you are already in a job and can get part-time work to boost your income. If your problems are more intransigent than that, then deferring the interest is likely to get you into even deeper water.

The possibility of capitalizing mortgage arrears is also mentioned. This means that the arrears would be added to the outstanding capital sum of your mortgage and you would repay them over the life of the loan. However, this option will increase your monthly repayments unless the repayment term is lengthened.

Finally, the option of equity-sharing arrangements, whereby another party (for example a housing association or property company) purchases a share of your property, is considered, although it is felt that these arrangements may be appropriate only in a small number of cases.

Borrowers are also encouraged to apply for any income support which may be available from the state. In particular, people who have recently fallen on hard times may be unaware of their social security rights and may be eligible for help. Check Appendix 1 to find the relevant sources of information.

The guidelines for mortgage lenders conclude that:

In the vast majority of cases these devices, together with the efforts of the borrower, are sufficient to prevent a minor arrears problem from becoming a major problem threatening possession. It is significant that while many people fall into arrears for a short time, under one per cent are over six months in arrears, and the number of possession cases is very much smaller.

What Happens If Your Home is Repossessed?

Repossession of your home is very much a last resort. If it does occur, it is likely to be with the agreement of the borrower. For example where some equity could be released and the borrower would benefit. In a minority of cases possession can take place because the borrower has simply abandoned his or her home and left it to the lender.

The lender will have to obtain a court order for repossession, and must do this according to a strict set of legal requirements. The 'possession order', as it is called, will be issued through the County Court, and will require a hearing, fixed some two months after the date of issue of the order. It is in the interests of the borrower to attend the hearing in order to make a case for the possession order not to proceed. The court could order the possession order be suspended, in return for the borrower's commitment to repay according to an agreed schedule. The court is likely to be sympathetic to the borrower's circumstances. However, the borrower must make every effort to abide by the new terms, otherwise the possession order might be reinstated.

In the event of the possession order being enforced, the lender is obliged to obtain the best possible price for the property within a reasonable time, and must pay the borrower any surplus after capital and arrears of interest have been deducted from the sale price.

Responsible lenders will also assist the borrower in liaising with the local authority's housing department to ensure that alternative housing is found. The local authority has a statutory duty to find accommodation for the ex-borrower.

The complete process of repossession of a mortgaged home is generally stressful and can result in marital problems, alcohol abuse and other negative symptoms. Yet there is absolutely no reason why this chain of events should occur as long as you maintain a cheerful, positive mental attitude and are determined to overcome your temporary problems. However, if you are in any doubt about your ability to pay the mortgage, then you must take action as early as possible to deal with the problem.

Rent Arrears

Rent arrears are very common, particularly with council housing, and many councils adopt a sympathetic attitude to tenants who have fallen into arrears through financial difficulties. Nevertheless, you should contact your housing officer or estate manager if you should fall into arrears. It may well be possible for you to repay these through a small addition to your regular rental payments. If the arrears are very large, and you are able to plead your case effectively, the council may even write them off.

Again, you would do well to seek help from your Citizen's Advice Bureau, Housing Aid centre, or even your MP. Another possibility is to move into smaller and cheaper accommodation through arranging an exchange with another council tenant. Check the bulletin boards on the estate, local newsagents, or local papers to find other council tenants willing to effect an exchange.

If you are in arrears to a private landlord, that person or company is likely to move very promptly to recover the money or to have you evicted for non-payment. You must be very careful to communicate with the landlord and try to reach an agreement for repayment. You might, for example, be able to negotiate on the basis of some repairs which need to be done—perhaps you could contribute your labour or materials in exchange for a reduction in the arrears. Whatever you do, do not avoid talking to the landlord.

If you persist in failing to pay rent, whether you are in the private or public sector, you will inevitably at some stage receive a notice to quit, followed by a court summons if no agreement can then be reached. The summons will include a 'form of admission' which you should complete and return to the court. The form will contain a section allowing you to plead your case.

As with mortgage arrears, you may be able successfully to argue your case, and retain your tenancy in exchange for repayments to the landlord. If you are counter-claiming for repairs or service deficiencies in your rented accommodation then you should apply for legal aid, again with the assistance of the Citizen's Advice Bureau or local authority Housing Aid centre.

You must beware of being evicted for non-payment of rent, particularly from council housing. You could be considered to be intentionally homeless, in which case it will be difficult to find alternative council housing. Private sector landlords will require references, and these will be difficult to get.

Arrears of Unsecured Loans

As we have already observed, arrears of unsecured loans are common, and lenders assume that a proportion of their borrowers will default. This does not mean that they will not take vigorous action to recover the debts.

In order to avoid court actions against you, or bailiffs knocking at the door, then you must observe the golden rule and contact your creditors. As part of your spending plan you will have identified already how much you can afford to pay to the banks and finance companies. The next step is to negotiate with each to ensure that they accept the terms of repayment.

How to Negotiate

You must find out whom to write to, preferably by name, and point out the following:

- That you fully intend to repay your outstanding debt.

- That you have worked out a plan to repay your debt.

- That all your creditors will be repaid an amount proportionate to your outstanding debt.

- That you can afford to pay x amount monthly.

Most reasonable creditors will respond in two ways: they will accept your offer (you are saving them considerable expense in chasing what would otherwise be a bad debt); and they will freeze the debt, not adding any further interest to it. If they will not freeze the debt at its current level (and you should ask them to do so) then at least they are likely to consider reducing the interest paid on the outstanding balance.

If you are dealing with an unreasonable company which continues to put pressure on you to pay more, you must resist. Send a cheque every month to the person with whom you are dealing—this keeps your relationship on a personal level, rather than a faceless transaction through a bank—and keep explaining that this is all you can afford.

It will help to convince unwilling creditors that you are serious if you give them the names and addresses of other creditors who have accepted your repayment plan. The fact that other companies are going along with your repayment schedule will allay suspicions that you are trying to swindle anyone. If you are persistent and steadfast, they will almost certainly give way.

Sample Letter to a Creditor

If you find it difficult to put pen to paper and write to those people to whom you owe money, then I suggest that you copy this letter (Table 10), adapting it to your circumstances, and send it off straight away. The longer you leave it the worse your debt problem will get, so remember the action principle and resolve to do it as soon as possible.

Table 10

A Customer
Rose Lane
Newtown
Berks

Tel. 0123 4455

XYZ Credit Co   3 May 1991
Moneylender Lane
London EC1

Dear (Name of the person, not just Sir or Madam)

I am writing to you in order to let you know that I have been finding it increasingly difficult to meet my monthly repayment obligations to your company.

However, I have recently resolved to put my financial affairs in order, and to follow a programme of strict budgeting. According to this programme, I have identified the amount of money which I can afford to repay your company each month. This is the sum of £X.

I have several other creditors, all of which are receiving payments in proportion to the amount of money owing to them. I would be happy to supply you with their names and addresses if you feel this would be useful.

Please note that should my income increase in the future, I will be able to increase the repayments.

I would be grateful if you would freeze the sum outstanding at its present level, so that I can repay it within a reasonable time.

Thank you for your help in this matter.

Yours sincerely

(Your name)

What If You End Up in Court?

Some people reading this book may already be so far down the road to chronic debt that they are already being threatened by creditors with court action. If you are in this situation now, or feel that you are likely to be in the near future, the first thing to remember is not to panic. Contact your creditors immediately and try to negotiate, even at this late stage, a realistic repayment schedule. Do this with professional help if necessary.

In the event that a creditor does not accept your offer of repayment at a level you can afford, and takes you to court, your good faith in paying what you can afford will favourably impress the magistrate. The law will almost certainly take your side and order the creditor to accept repayment terms which take account of your situation. Once the court judgement is made, the sum of money owed will in any case be frozen, and no further interest will be payable on it. Therefore, going to court could act in your favour if the creditor has so far refused to reduce the interest payable on the outstanding loan.

If you follow the principles outlined in this book, you will already be finding creative ways to reduce your expenses and increase your income. As your income increases you will find less and less difficulty in finding the money to meet your monthly repayments as time goes on.

Being Sued for Unsecured Debt

There are two basic means of suing a person for debt. The simplest is through the Small Claims Court, which is applicable for debts of less than £500. A claim is submitted to the court registrar who will hear the case and adjudicate the claim. There is no appeal once the judgement has been made.

Larger debts of up to £5000 are dealt with by the County Court. A summons will be issued which you must reply to within 14 days. The form sent along with the summons allows you to dispute the claim if you wish. A date will then be set by the court for the pre-trial hearing. This will be an informal meeting bringing creditor and debtor together in the hope that the dispute can be settled without further action. If the matter can be resolved, then the registrar will make a note of the agreement; this will be legally binding.

If you decide not to dispute the debt, you can either repay it within the 14 day period or ask the creditor to accept an offer. You will have to fill in the details of income, expenses and assets on the form. If the creditor does not agree to your offer, then the court will decide what should be the terms of repayment. As has already been noted, they are likely to be reasonable and not leave you penniless.

Dealing with Bailiffs

If a court order to pay according to an agreed schedule is ignored, then a distress warrant or warrant of execution will be issued against you. A bailiff will turn up on your doorstep without advance warning (sometime between Monday and Friday; they will not show up at the weekend), with the power to demand entry and to seize goods belonging to you which will be sold for a fraction of their value in order to discharge the debt.

If a bailiff does arrive, you should ask for identification and ask to see the distress warrant. You should remember that the bailiff is allowed to use 'reasonable force' to effect an entry should you refuse to let him or her in. You might also be charged with contempt of court should you resist.

The bailiff is not usually empowered to take goods that are not owned outright by you, such as those subject to rental or hire purchase agreements. If you have proof that certain goods are not owned by you, then it should be shown to the bailiff. If he takes goods not owned by you by mistake, you will still be liable for the loss to the finance company.

Attachment of Earnings Order

Another form of enforcement of repayment of arrears is an attachment of earnings order. This is often used to ensure payment of child maintenance, and lately it is one of an array of measures being introduced to ensure that people will pay their poll tax. Your employer will be required to deduct the necessary amount directly from your wages and pay it to the court. The court will then pay your creditors. Your employer is however under no legal obligation to co-operate with the order. If you can pluck up the courage to discuss your situation with your employer, your creditors may well have to find other ways of being repaid.

Also, an attachment of earnings order can only be enforced if you are in a stable job and have a stable address. If you frequently move and avoid communicating your name and address, you can stave off the day of reckoning. However, this is not really to be recommended.

Bankruptcy and What it Means

Bankruptcy is very much a last resort for a debtor, although often it is entered into voluntarily. It is a state that a debtor should take strenuous steps to avoid. Once bankrupted, you will be unable to lead a normal life for a minimum of two years, and sometimes longer. During this period you will have little income to live on, even if you are earning a good salary, as attachment of earnings orders will ensure that almost all of your income is gobbled up by creditors. Undoubtedly your family life will suffer, and you will quite probably be uprooted from your home.

Bankruptcy occurs usually when debts are in excess of £750 and the debtor is unable to pay. The creditor will have issued a statutory demand against the debtor, who will then have 21 days in which to decide whether to apply to have the demand set aside. There are various grounds for having a statutory demand set aside, such as if the debtor has a counter-claim against the creditor, or if there are other reasonable grounds for dispute.

If the statutory demand is not set aside, then the creditor will be allowed to serve a bankruptcy petition on the debtor. This will be followed by a court hearing, at which there is still time for an agreement to be made between debtor and creditor which will enable bankruptcy to be avoided.

Alternatively, a debtor can also present a petition to the court in order to declare voluntary bankruptcy. Whatever the source of the petition, once bankruptcy has been declared, the official receiver will take charge of all assets belonging to the bankrupt, except for essential tools of trade, clothing and bedding.

Once bankrupted, a person lives a controlled life financially. He or she can only have a bank account with the permission of the court, and this will not have a cheque card or overdraft facility. Any property belonging to the bankrupt will be sold within a year, although if it is in joint names the partner should be entitled to 50 per cent of the proceeds. The bankrupt will live more or less at subsistence level for two years, which is the normal period of bankruptcy for people whose estates are valued at less than £20,000.

Although for most people earning reasonable salaries bankruptcy should be avoided like the plague, it can be beneficial. For example, if you are already living at subsistence level and have a debt load which you cannot hope to repay, then it can be helpful to have the slate wiped clean and start again. However, most people would not want to have to go to these extremes. It is the purpose of this book to show that poverty and bankruptcy can be avoided if debtors are brave and willing to face up to their problems before the terminal stages of debt are reached.

If you are undergoing the ordeal of bankruptcy, then I am sure that you will already be climbing out of the abyss, facing the future with a positive mental attitude. At least you will know how *not* to get into such a state again!

Points to Remember

- Resolve to communicate with your creditors. Deal with secured debt first, then unsecured arrears.
- Deal with officials by name and be honest about your circumstances. A compromise will be reached. Creditors do not usually like to spend time and money taking debtors to court if it can be avoided.
- If you are threatened with court action, do not panic. Even at a late stage negotiations can be effected. The court may in any case be sympathetic.
- Understand the consequences of ignoring court orders made against you. Avoid bankruptcy at all costs, unless there really is no alternative.

STEP 8

Sell Surplus Assets

If you are fortunate enough to own possessions of substantial monetary value, yet are heavily in debt, one of the quickest ways of getting back to financial health is to sell what you have and start again—this time *saving* for depreciating possessions instead of borrowing for them.

Unfortunately, owing to the worldwide debt crisis which has caused a general economic downturn, the markets for many categories of goods are quite depressed, and this trend is likely to continue. During the early 1990s prices for such things as clothes, houses, cars and luxury goods have been falling. Instead of living with inflation, to which we had all grown so used, we are instead experiencing widespread deflation.

Only pensioners are likely to remember or believe that deflation—when prices actually fall in nominal terms—can happen. The last time this happened was in fact during the 1930s. Yet falling prices already have been a fact of life in the homes market, and have been a daily occurrence in commodity markets such as agricultural goods and minerals.

So, while you might want to think about selling your home, your car or some of your other expensive possessions to raise some cash, make sure you do not wind up selling at too much of a loss. If you sell at the right time, you may avoid the full effect of deflation.

I have been through this selling-off process, and I can assure you that it is a liberating experience. Instead of getting too emotionally attached to your possessions, and worrying about them, you can free yourself of the burden of ownership, when your possessions can end up owning you! Buddhists have long understood the dangers of too much pride in ownership, and it can be a relief to be free of major possessions, at least for a while.

It might seem a drastic step to take, but you might ask yourself this simple question. Is it better to be short of material possessions, and free of debt; or to be loaded with material goods, and yet up to your neck in debt? Only you know the answer to this question.

The basics of Selling

In our culture, at least until the Thatcher years, selling has tended to be frowned upon as a vulgar occupation. This disdain does not allow for the fact that everybody is involved in selling, even if they wish to pretend otherwise. Going to a job interview, negotiating with clients and customers, or seeking promotion within your firm are all sales activities. Selling is part of life.

However, nobody will buy anything, or be happy with it, if it was not what they wanted in the first place. Buying is a pleasure when you get what you want, and dealing with expert salespeople who are able to give you what you want is also a pleasure. Anyone who has bought a good suit of clothes sold by an enthusiastic salesperson knows this. We all like to feel we have got a good deal, and so we should. Both parties should feel that they have profited, for an efficient sale ensures mutual benefits for buyer and seller.

One thing is paramount in selling—you have to believe in the quality and value of the product. If you are selling something that is overpriced or of doubtful quality, it will be difficult to be enthusiastic about it. It is vital to be enthusiastic about the sale, as this mood is infectious and will almost certainly have a positive effect upon the buyer.

If you want to be successful in selling, one of the first things to remember is not to begin your spiel as soon as the customer expresses interest. Instead, you should ask as many questions as possible in order to understand exactly what the customer wants.

Once you have done this, then you can explain how the features and benefits of your goods already meet the customer's requirements, or can be adapted to meet them. It is no good trying to sell someone a Ford Fiesta if he or she is in the market for a Mercedes. If you don't make this mistake, you will avoid time-wasting, and will gain goodwill from your prospective customer, so that even if he or she decides not to buy your product, they may well know of someone who will.

When you sell anything, whether goods or services, it is also vital that you put yourself in the other person's shoes. That person, the potential buyer, or in the language of the sales professionals, the 'prospect', is concerned with only one set of criteria. That is, what *benefits* this purchase will bring him or her.

Unless you are already an expert salesman or have taken time off to study and practise the subject, you may think that selling is about explaining the features, of the goods or services. But this is only partly the case. You should be explaining how these features are translated into benefits.

Thus, if you are selling a luxury car, you might point out that it has ergonomically-designed seats, which probably won't mean much to the prospect until you explain that this feature means that your car is exceptionally comfortable to drive—an obvious benefit. If you are selling a cheaper model, you might like to point out that the engine is very economical, meaning that the prospect will save an average of £300 a year on petrol in comparison with rival models.

Turning features into benefits may require a bit of imagination. If there is some undesirable aspect of the product you are selling, you may have to 'paint a picture' in the mind's eye of the potential purchaser in order to turn the feature into a benefit. For example, your little kitchen could be transformed into a space-saving compact one, in which case you would have to explain how it could be transformed, and what benefits this would bring the purchaser. Remember, you are still selling value for money, as you will have allowed for a certain amount of bargaining over the less-desirable features of the item.

Volumes have been written on sales technique. However, the basics can be learned in a couple of hours, and there are sales seminars available to teach you them. After that you need lots of practice. The money invested in a competent sales seminar will soon be returned to you, so it really is worth making the effort to learn how to sell effectively.

Selling Your Home

Few people go about selling their homes with a light heart. The process is undoubtedly stressful, not least because the archaic laws of the UK (except Scotland) make it so, in that negotiations can drag on for many months before completion of the sale. There is also the emotional attachment people feel to their homes, and the administrative difficulties involved in moving.

There are, however, powerful financial arguments for selling your home, especially if you find that paying the mortgage is a struggle and if you are not too emotionally attached to the property. Falling property prices mean that the equity you have built up in the property during the 1970s and 1980s will be eroded during the 1990s. House prices should continue to fall until they are once again in line with people's ability to pay.

This process will continue for some years to come. When it is completed, a great many people will find that the equity built up in their homes during the 1980s has evaporated. Latecomers to the house price boom have already discovered this sad fact of life in the 1990s.

Instead of enduring falling profits, you can take them and invest your money more appropriately. The interest earned on the money can be reinvested, or can offset your rental payments while preserving your capital.

If, for example, you have a £30,000 mortgage on a house worth £85,000; £50,000 or more could be realized from the sale of your property after estate agent's, solicitor's and removals' fees have been deducted. If this sum is invested in a bank or building society high-interest account it will generate an after-tax annual income of approximately £5,000 a year.

Assuming you can rent a property for, say, £100 a week, your actual rent bill will be next to nothing. This compares with the cost of the £30,000 mortgage, which would be around £3,500 a year, to which rates and repair bills would have to be added. Thus, until property falls to a level where renting again begins to look unattractive, you might well feel that continuing to pay off a mortgage on a property in which you have substantial equity, but which continues to fall in price, is not really sensible.

The first thing to realize about selling your home is that most estate agents couldn't sell fur coats to Eskimos. Some of them are quite good at *showing* people your property (although some can barely even manage this!), but few actually attempt to *sell* it. You are pretty much on your own here, so it is worth having taken the time to learn the basics of selling.

The first thing to do is to prepare a full set of particulars about your house or flat. Agents are supposed to do this, but sometimes they will send round potential purchasers without the details. Also, you should check agents' details carefully. They will occasionally make mistakes in room measurements, lopping a couple of feet off the length or width. Often they neglect to mention features of the property, such as plentiful power points, or a good aspect. Rarely will they stress the benefits deriving from these features.

Having your own written description of the property shows that you are organized and enthusiastic, and that impresses people. One of the tenets of selling is that the customer has got to like you if you want to make the sale, and demonstrating enthusiasm and efficiency is going to help the prospect warm to you.

A comprehensive set of particulars stressing both features and benefits will also help to make your property stand out in the mind of the prospective buyer long after he or she has actually visited your home.

The second point to remember is that you want the property advertised as widely as possible, which means putting it with a large number of agents. It is invariably a false economy to choose a sole agency, unless that agency is exceptionally efficient. The difference in fees paid for multiple agencies rather than just one is not large, usually one to one-half of a percentage point. It is not really worth being niggardly, if you want your property to sell.

You might also consider putting an advertisement in the local paper yourself for a month or so before placing the house with estate agents. This is not very expensive, even if you get a display advertisement. Some prospective buyers believe that they will get a better deal from a private sale, in that the seller can allow them a discount to reflect the commission he or she would otherwise have had to pay to an agent. Anyway, the general idea is to get as many potential purchasers as possible to hear about your property, which means that you don't skimp on advertising.

Pricing is often a problem. Chances are that the agents you consult will have quite a range of opinions as to how much your home is worth. For example, I sold my London flat just past the peak of the market when estimates of its worth ranged from £100,000 to £125,000; a considerable variation. In fact, the lower estimates were correct, as we were just beginning to enter a bear market with its consequent falling prices. When prices are rising, you may get offers at the top end of the range. Assuming we are still in a bear market (with falling prices) when you sell, the trick is to price the flat realistically, as the agents say. If people believe that they are getting a bargain, then they are likely to buy quickly and willingly, and your house won't stay long on the market.

A noticeable feature of the changed market situation has been that buyers are prone to take their time, and to view a lot of properties before they settle on their ideal home. So you will have to get used to a lot of people traipsing in an out of your home, which can be annoying. You'll just have to grin and bear it, and keep working at selling the place.

The effort you go to in order to make your house or flat an inviting place to inspect does have a bearing on the buyer's mood, and hence on the likely prospects of a sale. If you can make the exterior look as attractive as possible, with a new coat of paint or flowers in the garden, then your chances of making a good impression will be enhanced. Make sure that the front porch is swept, that the garden is tidy, and that the path is not overgrown with weeds.

If you live in an urban property without a garden, why not invest in some window boxes? Fresh flowers inside the house also make for a cheerful atmosphere, especially in a room with a somewhat gloomy aspect, or in the kitchen or bathroom, which do not usually get so much attention.

Good lighting is also extremely important, especially on grey winter days. Turn on the lights *before* the rooms are inspected, and experiment with improving a room's mood using table lamps. If you have an open fireplace and want to make a winter house look more cheerful, do light a fire. Some agents also reckon that the smell of bread baking or percolating coffee (and the offer of a cup) works wonders for a sale! It all helps to make your property stand out from the competition.

A lot of the above suggestions may seem like common sense, but it is amazing how many vendors neglect to make such improvements. Make the extra effort to impress the buyer and you will be rewarded with a quicker sale at a better price. You don't have to spend a fortune—but do use your imagination and energy.

Securing the Sale

Before securing a buyer, you should already have arranged to have a competent solicitor to organize conveyancing for you. Specialist conveyancing firms may well be your best bet, and can be a lot cheaper than your neighbourhood solicitor. Fees charged by the latter can easily be twice as much as those charged by the specialists. Like everything else, it pays to shop around and get a number of different quotes.

One other word of caution. During the 1980s property boom, 'gazumping' was common, where would-be buyers found themselves outbid by newcomers. This practice has given way to 'gazundering', which is the opposite, whereby buyers threaten to pull out at the last minute unless the vendor reduces the price.

There seems to be only one solution to this practice—keep showing the property to other prospects right up until the time contracts are exchanged. That way, you keep the pressure on the buyer and safeguard yourself from timewasters.

Selling your home in a bear market cannot be said to be easy, and is often a frustrating experience. However, keep at it and eventually you will be successful. There are plenty of people out there who still believe that property is the best investment, despite the occasional overwhelming evidence to the contrary.

In my own view, property prices are likely to fall substantially during the 1990s. Even conservative estimators consider that falls of up to 20 per cent in real terms (adjusted for inflation) will be necessary to bring house prices into line with realistic multiples of income. Prices should be around two and a half times average incomes, whereas at the peak of the last housing boom they were close to five times average incomes.

Those of us who consider that housing has been the subject of a speculative mania would predict even more of a decline. A fall of 50 per cent or more on prices ruling in mid-1988 is not beyond the realms of possibility as the long-term economic cycle is played out and real incomes begin to fall. Only if you are completely solvent and confident of your continuing ability to repay the mortgage should you be relaxed about this prospect, however remote you may believe it to be.

In the meantime, estate agents, building society spokespeople, and others with a vested interest in the property market will continue to assure us that prices will begin to rise again soon. Some people will believe these pundits, and will buy back into the market at the wrong time; or will refuse to sell in the anticipation of a renewed bull market in housing, when prices rise quickly. There may well be small rallies in the market during the 1990s, particularly when interest rates eventually fall, and many people will take these as signs of a new bull market. These rallies will be short-lived, however, and will not change the overall deflationary trend. You may be able to take advantage of one of these mini-rallies to get out of the housing market.

Selling at Auction

It may be tempting for you to consider selling your home at auction, especially if you want a quick sale. During the bull market in property, with prices rising fast, auctions became increasingly popular as a means of effectively valuing property, particularly if it was unusual property.

Traditionally, however, auctions have been places for selling in a hurry, and have attracted property developers and speculators who have been looking for bargains. This is especially true during a bear market. There is also no guarantee that you will sell the property, even at a poor price relative to that which you might have sold it for through an estate agent.

If you do decide to sell at auction, it is best to have a realistic reserve price, which will be 10 to 20 per cent below the price you expect to actually get. You will have to ensure that the title deeds are available to the buyer, although in other respects it is a case of *caveat emptor*, Latin for 'let the buyer beware!' The prospective owner should also have made all the relevant checks before concluding the purchase.

Selling Your Car

Fortunately, unless you own a heap of junk, selling a car is a lot easier than selling a house. Much the same principles apply, however. You will want to advertise the vehicle as widely as possible, with the *Exchange and Mart* (or similar sales paper) and your own local paper being excellent media for this. Make your advertisement stand out from all the others by having it printed in bold type or put in a box. Offer value for money and you should get a fair number of enquiries.

It is worth making the effort to clean both the exterior and the interior of the car, and make sure that all the tyres are correctly inflated, including the spare. If the vehicle is temperamental and difficult to start, then get the problem sorted out, or at least keep the engine warmed up. There is nothing that puts a buyer off more than a car that won't start, even if he or she is a DIY fan. A buyer is going to want to negotiate quite a bit off the price if the car is obviously problematic.

Selling a car at auction is also worth considering. There are plenty of auctions about, but you will probably not get a good price if your car is in good condition. Slightly unreliable vehicles are likely to do better with this method.

Personally, I am not keen on sales or trade-ins with professional car dealers. Unless you are an absolutely brilliant negotiator with a good knowledge of what you are selling or buying, you are not likely to get a good price from professional dealers.

Furniture and Household Goods

You may be tempted to get rid of some of your furniture and large household appliances. By all means sell-off the stuff you don't want, but I would not advise selling good furniture and appliances that you like and need. You are unlikely to get anything like the replacement value; it is a better idea to hold on to good-quality household goods for as long as possible, even putting them in storage for a time if you have sold your house.

If you are going to sell household goods, the small ads in your local paper are a good outlet. Smaller items could also be sold at car boot sales, which are gaining increasing popularity, attract large numbers of buyers looking for bargains, and are cheap to enter.

During an economic slump, retailers will start dumping new furniture and household appliances on the market at previously unheard-of bargain prices. If you are able to mobilize as much cash as possible now, you will benefit from these bargains. In the years ahead, cash raised from the sale of major assets like your house or car is likely to buy quite a lot more than it does now.

Jewellery and Other Valuables

It is often problematic emotionally to dispose of jewellery and other valuables such as family heirlooms. Often, such things are not merely possessions; they embody the spirit of the people and places with which they are associated. So it is not always a good idea to sell them unless you are genuinely emotionally detached from them.

Gold and silver valuables should be worth whatever the weight of the metal within them at current bullion prices. However, a specialist dealer might not always give you full value. The antiques and jewellery markets are likely to remain quite depressed, in which case it will be hard to get good prices.

An alternative would be to leave the valuables as collateral with a pawnbroker, and receive a loan in exchange. Pawnbrokers are again doing good business after having been considered rather old-fashioned. This will be a secured loan, and you will have to pay interest on it. As another form of debt, it is not really to be encouraged.

Endowment Policies

If you are considering cashing in a with-profits endowment policy to release capital for debt repayment, then it is important for you to realize that the amount you will be paid by the insurance company issuing the policy is unlikely to reflect its true with-profits value. This is especially true if you cash in a policy in its early years. The company will deduct commission and administration costs, and will not be bound to pay bonuses until the policy is fully paid-up over the agreed length of the term. Thus the surrender value offered by the company for your policy will rarely reflect its true market value.

It is possible to get a better price for your policy by selling it to another individual or institution. This can be done through a broker or an auctioneer. You should get some 15 to 20 per cent more for your policy by selling it through an intermediary than by surrendering it directly to the insurance company. Some names and addresses of organizations offering a broking or auction service are given in Appendix 1.

Points to Remember

- Selling surplus assets is a quick way to cancel unwanted debts.
- Take the time to learn how to sell. Sell the benefits of the product as well as its features.
- Selling your home is a more difficult emotional decision. However, do not assume that house price inflation will come back in the 1990s.
- Renting is a feasible alternative to paying off a mortgage, especially if you have built up substantial equity in your home.
- Consider selling your car if you feel you could do without it. Otherwise trade down to a cheaper vehicle.
- It is often difficult to get good prices for second-hand furniture, household appliances and most jewellery. Sell only what you don't want or need.

PART 3
Achieving Prosperity

With money in the bank, you are wise, you are handsome, and you sing well too!

— *Yiddish proverb*

STEP 9

Increase Your Income

So far you have made concrete progress in understanding the root causes of debt, and know how to tackle the debt habit head-on by recording and planning your expenditure. Now it is necessary to go one step further and identify opportunities for increasing your income, so that your debt can be eliminated that much more quickly. It is not usually very difficult to find ways of increasing one's income, no matter what the situation. Just as for getting out of debt, the major ingredients are a positive mental attitude allied to determination, persistence and careful planning.

Know Yourself

It is important to begin the task of identifying extra income-earning opportunities by taking stock of your strengths and weaknesses. In doing this, it is helpful to list on paper what you believe are your personal abilities. You will be looking to maximize your strengths and minimize exposure to your weaknesses thereby increasing your chances of success. You will need to carry out this exercise in regard to both your character and your work experience.

The daily practise of meditation will help enormously. In common with most things in life, the more effort you put into meditation the more benefits you will extract. The daily period of quiet and reflection will help your subconscious mind to remind you of the tasks you are good at and what opportunities there might be to exploit your talents and strengths. If you are not sure what your abilities really are, then meditation will help to reveal them.

Other valuable sources of information about your abilities and what you want from a job are your partner, sympathetic members of your family, or close friends. Having as they do, a degree of detachment, they should be able to assist you in defining your strengths and weaknesses clearly. Thus you will have the raw material with which to identify opportunities that might be open to you.

When looking for income-earning opportunities, you must drop any pre-conceived ideas of being trained to do only certain jobs. You must also suspend ideas about certain jobs being too high or too low in status for you. If you are serious about getting out of debt as quickly as possible, any extra income, no matter how derived, is going to make a tremendous difference. Equally, if you are already in a poorly paid job or are unemployed, you should not be afraid to aim high in the quest for an improvement in your income and/or job prospects.

In common with a key principle discussed earlier in this book, your urgent need to increase income, which some people might consider to be a 'problem', can instead be viewed as an opportunity. You will be able to re-orientate your life towards more enjoyable and fulfilling work, both enhancing your income and improving your emotional life.

Enjoying Your Occupation

It follows logically from what is said above that you should make strenuous efforts to find work you enjoy. After all, you spend almost half your waking hours working. Yet many people hate their work. If you are in this category, you know what it feels like to loathe getting up in the morning, to watch the clock at the workplace, and to rush home at the end of the working day.

You will never fulfil your real potential in a job you hate. You will never reach your personal earning targets unless you enjoy your work, and believe in what you are doing. Consequently, you will need to plan your escape.

It is likely to be impossible or impractical for you to leave your job right away, particularly if you are heavily in debt, or if the economy is looking uncertain. A more practical immediate alternative might be to find different work within your current organization which you might enjoy more. Otherwise, you might decide to develop a more positive attitude towards your work. There are bound to be some enjoyable aspects of your employment—you can concentrate on doing these better, and taking more pride in what you do.

If the major part of your dislike for work resides in your relationships with people around you, then perhaps you can find ways around that too. Ask your subconscious mind for the answers, and your life will swiftly become more bearable.

If you are thinking to yourself: 'it's all very well for him—I live in a high unemployment area where there just aren't enough jobs to go around'—then consider the following.

If you do something you enjoy, then you will do it well. If you do the job well, whether it is making a product or providing a service, then it will be a product or service of quality. How many times do you really come across a quality product or service, or both? What do you think would happen if you were able to provide quality? The world would beat a path to your door—that's what!

People will pay a premium for quality. Customers who have been the victim of shoddy goods and services will never come back to the supplier of those goods and services. Customers who expect, and get, excellent quality will keep coming back and will tell their friends and relatives. Employees whose work is of a consistently high quality should not fear unemployment, they will be valued members of the organization and will be retained at the expense of others, unless there is a complete closure of the company or department.

There are thousands of builders in this country. Almost everyone has a horror story to tell about 'cowboy' builders. Yet there are a few very good builders who make an extremely good living. They never have to advertise and they usually have more work than they can handle— and they are certainly not the cheapest.

Find the work you love to do, and you won't be short of customers. This is true whether you are an employer or an employee. Even if you live in a high unemployment area you can find ways to meet local needs better; or to serve customers in more prosperous regions. Go for quality goods and services offering value for money and you will flourish.

Part-time Opportunities

Given the urgency of increasing your income, your first thought will almost certainly be to look for ways of increasing your income through part-time work. The key point here is to be flexible, taking advantage of a wide variety of opportunities which exist even in the depths of the worst economic slump.

If you live in a part of the country which does not seem to offer much in the way of formal part-time employment, then you are going to have to consider not only those vacancies paying a defined wage, but those which involve working on a commission basis. Most of these will be sales jobs of one kind or another. Many people are afraid of selling and automatically reject these opportunities. Yet this is often a mistake, as the rewards can often be much higher than those offered by ordinary part-time jobs.

If you are going to sell a product or service, it is best to avoid those 'business opportunities' which involve your buying stock and then selling it at a higher price. If you are thinking of doing this, then you must check out the product or service very carefully indeed in order to make sure it is really worth the effort. Unfortunately, there are a lot of companies around which rely on selling junk products to distributors on the promise of astronomical earnings from their resale. All too often these products turn out to be too highly priced or of inferior quality, and are therefore difficult to sell. A better route to take is to approach companies which do sell superior products and ask if you can act as an agent for them. You don't necessarily have to knock on doors—it is often better to use referrals from existing 'satisfied customers', who might at first be your friends and relatives.

Another way of boosting your income is to make a product and sell it yourself. This way you can offer excellent value for money as there is no middle-man. This could be anything from dressmaking to window-cleaning.

If you own physical assets, such as a car or a home, then you might consider using these to make money. Car owners will have opportunities such as taxi-driving open to them; and will be well placed to become part-time salespeople. Home owners who have extra space available may want to let out a room on a permanent or seasonal basis. Privacy may be somewhat affected, but the income derived from the lodgers could be quite substantial.

It may also be worth investing in a training course at night school in order to pick up skills and qualifications which can be turned into cash. For example, there is at the moment a boom in alternative health therapies which are virtually recession-proof in that most people are willing to pay for improved health. Massage, nutrition counselling, stress management and the like are all fruitful areas in which a modest investment of time and money could reap a good financial return.

Again, if you want extra paid employment, then apart from applying for the vacancies which are advertised, which might be few and far between, you are going to have to exercise initiative and imagination.

Check Your Entitlement to State Benefits

It is sometimes overlooked by people under financial strain that the State offers a considerable array of benefits to people on low incomes.

Some of these are well known, mostly automatic entitlements; but others are discretionary and must be applied for. Some 25 per cent of the people who are entitled to claim State benefits each year do not in fact do so. It is certainly worth checking up on your benefit entitlements.

The Department of Social Security (DSS) publishes a booklet entitled 'Which Benefit' which is available from post offices, DSS offices, or Citizen's Advice Bureaux.

Having said this, it must be added that claiming State benefits is a bit of a chore. It can be quite demeaning, what with all the forms to fill in, containing questions about your income and willingness to work. The offices are usually crowded, the queues lengthy, and the staff overworked. Once you are claiming benefits, you will find it difficult to keep them if you work even on a part-time basis. While it is important to check your eligibility, you should be looking to improve your financial situation through finding well paid full- or part-time employment as rapidly as possible.

Research the Hidden Job Market

Only a small proportion of jobs are actually advertised. The majority of posts are filled by candidates already identified and recruited. Some of these people are from within the organization, others are brought in as a result of recommendations from people known to the employer.

You can increase your chances of finding extra or better employment dramatically by looking out for unadvertised vacancies. You will not only be able to discover extra jobs, but you will be competing with far fewer applicants to get the available positions. However, in order to be successful, you must see yourself literally as a product to be sold effectively.

In order to market and sell yourself efficiently you will have to prepare and plan carefully. Marketing yourself means finding the right employment opportunities; while selling yourself means getting offered the jobs. You will have already identified the skills, experience and aptitudes you have to offer. Next you must identify which firms are likely to need your skills. Then you will need to find out who are the decision-makers in those firms, and approach them. Finally, you must effectively sell yourself to them if a vacancy has arisen, or you must ask for referrals to people who might be in a position to employ you.

In devising your personal marketing plan, you are going to have to do a fair amount of research to cast the net as widely as possible. Your local Chamber of Commerce might help you to identify which firms are expanding and are likely to need extra help. Similarly, you will need to register with the Job Centre for the employment opportunities they can provide. Assistance from people in your industry, or from people you know in other industries, is likely to prove invaluable. They will have intimate knowledge of which firms are doing well; and whom to approach.

As noted previously, you do not have to restrict yourself only to areas of employment in which you have experience. Choose others in which you can demonstrate relevant ability or enthusiasm. For example, if you are an office clerk by profession, but enjoy DIY at home, there is nothing to stop you applying for the position of part-time maintenance worker at the local hostel, provided that you can fit it around your existing work schedule.

Similarly, if you have zero experience but lots of enthusiasm, persistence will get you the job you want. One of my favourite examples of this was an acquaintance who left school with very little in the way of paper qualifications but who was determined to work in a bank. She found out the name of the manager of the branch in which she wanted to gain employment, and rang him up every day until he agreed to interview her. Having developed a friendly relationship on the phone, she was off to a good start. She was offered a job, and turned out to be a model employee.

When researching the hidden job market, one of the most useful ways to approach people is to ask for advice on how to go about getting a job, rather than bluntly asking for one. The people you approach will often be flattered to be consulted, and will usually take the time to see you. Most people who are in a position to help will do everything they can to assist an enthusiastic person. Also, meeting people in this way is good practice for interviews.

Prepare a Short CV

No matter what job you are going for, whether it is full-time or part-time, professional or manual work, it is important to prepare a short *curriculum vitae* (CV), or work history. This should not exceed two pages in length, unless you are going for a highly technical job for which more details are required. You may in this case wish to prepare two CVs, one to secure initial interviews, and another to follow up successful applications.

A CV should begin with basic information about yourself, followed by a statement of your work objective. Relevant work experience, such as your current or last position should appear on the first page. Any qualifications can be relegated to a second page. There is no need to give the names of referees until you are under serious consideration for the position.

An example is given in Table 11.

Table 11: Sample CV

Personal Details
Name: P Byrne   *Date of Birth:* 7.11.59
Nationality: British   *Marital Status:* Married, 2 children
Address: 2 Sunny Terrace, Newtown, NT12 1AA
Telephone: (0101) 44979

Career Objective
Having worked as an engineering fabrication foreman for five years, I am now seeking a managerial position in an engineering firm or similar establishment which will give me scope to develop my managerial skills.

Work History
1986-present: Supervisor with Brown Brothers Engineers Ltd, Industry Road, Newtown. My duties include assistance with pricing of quotations, quality control, and general supervision of work on projects up to £1 million in value. I am in charge of a group of ten skilled workers.

1980-86:   Welder with Turner Fabrications Ltd, Oldtown. I worked on a wide variety of engineering projects, and received further training in advanced welding techniques, including certification to code ASME 9.

Qualifications
1979-80:   Newtown Technical College

City and Guilds certificate in Welding Engineering Craft Studies: parts 1, 2 and 3.

1974-78:   Newtown Comprehensive School

CSE English, Maths, Technical Drawing, Physics, Woodwork, History, Geography.

I received a school prize for technical drawing.

Leisure Interests
Angling (Secretary of Newtown Angling Club), car racing and maintenance (competitor at local and national meetings).

Referees
Available on request.

There are a number of further points to be noted about the preparation
of an effective CV. First of all it must not be long-winded. It should,
however, include any quantifiable information that indicates successes
or responsibilities. It is likely that you will be able to find quite a lot of
positive things to say about your present position or past jobs. Try to
put this information across in some measurable way, such as 'I
increased sales by 30 per cent within a year', or 'I reduced
manufacturing costs by an average of 10 per cent per annum'.

If you have been unemployed for some time and do not wish to draw
attention to this fact, then it might help to leave out the dates of your
employment and instead write about your job experience and
responsibilities. The same would be true of a failed business venture.
Any queries about dates of past employment can be dealt with at the
interview, where you will have less chance of being rejected.
Remember that the main function of the CV is to act as a marketing
tool to get you interviews. You will be able to sell yourself further once
you have got them.

It is also important to consider that your leisure activities can be used
as an opportunity to demonstrate to a prospective employer that you
are enthusiastic, responsible and go-ahead. Any positions of authority,
such as acting as a club official or even organizing the local church
fête should be included. If you have decided to go for a job closely
related to your leisure interests, then you can use these as examples
of relevant experience.

In the CV shown in Table 11, Mr Byrne could have decided that he
would rather work as a car mechanic than a welder. In this case, he
would change the wording of the career objective to suit the
application, drawing attention to his success as a motor racing
enthusiast in his spare time.

Career histories should always be typed, although the letters
accompanying them can be hand written. The beauty of a short CV
is that it can easily be adapted to suit the job for which you are
applying. This is made easier still if you have access to a word
processor.

You will need at least two referees, who should be approached beforehand. It may seem obvious that you should pick people who both know you well and who will give a favourable impression, but you may like to check that they will indeed be saying kind things about you. Also, don't forget to thank your referees once you have been successful and have landed an appointment.

Selling Yourself at the Interview

An effective CV, carefully written and targeted, will soon land you interviews. You must then plan to succeed in the interview as carefully as you have planned the rest of your job campaign.

It is an established fact that potential employers make up their minds about applicants very rapidly, often within five minutes or so of their having entered the room. Therefore, you must make every effort to ensure that your appearance is correct for the job. Even small details, such as the condition of your shoes, your posture, and your hair-style can make the difference between automatic rejection or interest. In general, therefore, it is not a good idea to be too scruffy and outrageous unless you are applying for a job where you are expected to be unconventional, and there cannot be too many of those outside the pop music and fashion industries!

I have applied for jobs in several different industries. It never fails to fascinate me just how varied are the ways in which corporate culture is expressed. Each organization has a definite style of dress, vocabulary and even mannerism. If you wish to be successful, you must become a chameleon and emulate the people who are interviewing you. People like people who are like themselves.

Once you have appeared to be an acceptable type of person to the organization, it could be said that you are over the major hurdle. Nevertheless, you will still need to be briefed as much as possible about the organization. You will need to know what it does, what its turnover is, what its prospects are, and what difficulties and opportunities it is facing. You will have an opportunity to show off your knowledge either directly, such as in answer to the question 'how much do you know about this company?', or indirectly when you are asked some other question by managing to slip in the facts you have gathered.

Again it is important to appear relaxed and in control at the interview. It is fine to take notes, which shows interest. Have a few questions to ask to show an intelligent interest in the firm. Smile and address the interviewers by name to show that you are interested in them. Rehearse any difficult questions you may be asked. A favourite with interviewers is 'what do you think you can offer this organization?'. If you haven't worked out how your skills and experience should be presented, then you might flounder at a crucial moment.

One topic to be wary of is your attitude to past employers. When asked for your views about your current job or work history, on no account must you be negative about the experience, especially if you have suffered from bad personal relationships. Otherwise, you will give the impression that you are disruptive or negative yourself, no matter how justified you may feel your grievances to be.

Part of your preparation should be to run through with your partner or a friend all the major questions you might be asked, and to develop good answers for them. Your assistant could help you to practise by acting as the interviewer. In this way you are likely to be less nervous when interviewed.

Do not forget the programming you can feed to your subconscious mind to ensure interview success. Affirmations and visualization can help enormously with interviews. The more prepared and relaxed you are, the more likely you are to be successful. This is especially the case when you are chasing a job which has not yet been advertised. If the interviewer believes that you are the right person for the job, then you will have saved the company the trouble and expense of formal methods of recruitment.

Points to Remember

- If you are in unsuitable full-time employment, either because you don't enjoy it or you feel that it doesn't pay enough, then take action now to change that situation.
- Identify your main strengths and weaknesses, and try to find work which will best use your abilities and experience.
- If you want to speed up the process of debt elimination, you must make strenuous efforts to get extra income. Part-time employment is the first thing to look for.
- Do not discount acting as a sales representative for reputable products, as this may provide a better return on effort than conventional employment. Do consider selling your own products or services.

- Check your eligibility for State benefits.
- The hidden, unadvertised job market is a rich source of opportunity with little direct competition from other job seekers. Seek advice from knowledgeable people to tap into this market.
- Design a short curriculum vitae to use as a marketing tool to secure interviews.
- Prepare carefully for the interview by finding out as much as possible about the organization. Dress appropriately and ask intelligent questions. Remember that first impressions are the most important.

STEP 10

Learn how to save and invest

When you started reading this book, your thoughts were probably a long way away from the subject of investment! For someone deeply in debt, saving may seem an impossibility. However, having read this far, you are equipped to practise, and I hope are already practising the principles of debt elimination and income enhancement.

The purpose of this final part of the book is to launch you even further along the road to prosperity by outlining the basic principles of saving and investment, so that you may better identify your goals and ensure a prosperous future as well as a prosperous present.

The nature and principle of saving

You will remember that at the outset it was explained that debt respects no one. People on £100,000 a year can be just as badly in debt as people on £10,000 a year, both in absolute terms and as a proportion of their incomes.

The principle of saving is similar to the principle of debting, although it is its obverse. Just as the debtor debts, regardless of his or her income, so the saver saves, regardless of income. As getting into debt is a habit, so is saving. The principle of saving is straightforward. It is to *decide on the proportion of your income that you are going to save, and to save it regardless of day-to-day circumstances!*

Now, the compulsive debtor, or the person who manages only to break even each month, is likely to say that this is impossible. There always seems to be some unforeseen emergency, leading them to spend more than is necessary. The majority of such people fully intend to save, but find that by the end of the month there is nothing left, or even that there is a deficit.

The secret of the savings habit is to save *at the beginning of the month or week in which one is paid*. This money is sacrosanct, not to be touched except for investment purposes. The money saved should be put in its own account, preferably one in which the money is not instantly accessible.

Whatever is left, you will live on. You will simply adjust your expenditure to meet your new standard of living. From your spending record and spending plan you will have identified where economies might reasonably be made without compromising your way of life. Your spending plan, should, in fact include a savings plan, to get you into the savings habit as soon as possible!

For the person who is already in debt and paying off creditors, I would suggest that 5 per cent of your *net income* (after deductions such as tax and National Insurance) should be saved, as long as there is room for this in the household budget. For the person who 'breaks even' each month, 10 per cent of *gross income* (before deductions), is the recommended target.

This may seem a lot, but I promise you, after a short time you will hardly notice the difference. You will also enjoy the comfortable money-in-the-bank feeling which enhances your personal security and self-esteem.

Saving for Emergencies

You will already have understood from your spending record that emergencies are rarely true emergencies. Those previously unforeseen repair bills, clothing requirements, birthday presents, parties, visits to relatives, days off sick etc can be budgeted for, because you know from your spending record with what frequency they are likely to occur. Your spending record will allow you to plan for future 'emergencies'.

Again it is a good idea to keep such money separate from your current account, which is for everyday expenditure, and from your savings account, which is for investment. Open a third instant access account which pays a good rate of interest. When you need money for car insurance, a season ticket, a TV licence, dancing lessons or a birthday present, you may withdraw it from this account or transfer it to your current account.

The amount you need for extras and emergencies can be calculated from your spending record. Divide the annual amount by 12 or by 52, depending on whether you get paid weekly or monthly, and put this in the account every month. I would recommend adding a 10 per cent margin to the amount calculated on your spending plan. This will allow for any genuine emergencies which you could not have foreseen.

Once the money starts going into your account on a regular basis, you will begin to build up a small surplus. This can be used at the end of the year as a float giving you an extra financial cushion next year. It could otherwise be added to your investment account, or simply used to treat yourself to a holiday or a present as a reward for being so organized and disciplined.

When you calculate the amount you need to meet extra expenses weekly or monthly, you will probably be appalled! It may well be as much as 20 per cent of your income. However, if that is what your spending record tells you, then it will certainly be the case. The act of putting such a large proportion of your income aside each pay-day will also help you to cut down further on unnecessary expenditure, or make you to think twice about running the risk of avoidable emergencies, such as parking tickets.

On the other hand, the surplus you begin to enjoy from these economies may well be used to further enhance your life-style. Whatever happens, your spending will be firmly under control, and you will have begun your regular savings plan. Let us now consider the staggering rewards open to the dedicated saver.

The Rewards of Saving

You will remember from previous chapters that when you borrow money, the power of compound interest is working *against* you, piling up horrific extra amounts of money on top of your original debt. The longer the term of the loan, the more you end up repaying. In the case of a house, for example, you are likely to repay at least three times more than the actual purchase price by the time the loan has been paid off.

When you are a saver and an investor, the power of compound interest begins to work *for* you. Just how powerful this can be is illustrated below.

The Magic of Compound Interest

The ability of money to multiply through the power of compound interest has been called a 'magical' property. This can be seen from the examples given in Table 12. If you save £100 now, at a net interest rate of 10 per cent, which is easily achievable at current interest rates, over various time periods your money will grow as shown:

Table 12: £100 Invested at 10 per cent Compound Over Different Time Periods:

5 years	£ 161.05
10 years	£ 259.37
15 years	£ 417.72
20 years	£ 672.75
25 years	£1083.47
30 years	£1744.94

Quite a respectable sum can be accumulated. As we would expect, the longer the time period, the more money is made. However, through compound interest, the growth rate of the money invested accelerates over time, so that the difference between the sum accumulated between say 20 and 25 years—£410.95—is much greater than that between, say 10 and 15 years, when your money grows by only £158.35.

Now let us look at what happens when we begin saving £100 *per month* over the same period of time. See Table 13.

Table 13: £100 per Month Accumulated Over 30 Years at an Interest Rate of 10 per cent Compound per Annum:

5 years	£ 7,907
10 years	£ 20,750
15 years	£ 41,877
20 years	£ 76,630
25 years	£133,797
30 years	£227,837

The sums accumulated now are quite staggering. By the end of ten years, you will have cash assets worth more than £21,000. After 25 years (the traditional period of mortgage repayment, for example) the money saved will be worth well over £133,000.

Only five short years later, your money will have grown by *a further* £94,000, to reach a total of £227,837. All through the principle of regular saving allied to the magic of compound interest.

Net versus Gross Interest Reinvested

Just as the length of time over which you leave your money to accumulate interest makes a dramatic difference to the final figure, so too does a few points difference in the interest rate. Just consider, by way of illustration, the difference in amounts accumulated if interest is paid gross, rather than having tax deducted. In Table 14, we assume a 3-point difference, with gross interest being 13 per cent.

Table 14:   £100 per Month Invested at a Gross Interest Rate of 13 per cent:

5 years	£ 8,579
10 years	£ 24,762
15 years	£ 55,687
20 years	£114,589
25 years	£227,079
30 years	£441,768

As you can see, the difference in the final figures on Tables 13 and 14 is rather large—£213,927, to be exact. It is interesting to note not only that a relatively small difference in the interest rate makes a large difference to the final figure, but also that by the last two years of saving your money is growing by nearly £50,000 a year!

Please note also that in the above examples the amount saved monthly has not been increased, whereas in reality it would most probably be increased annually as your income rises.

By now I am sure that you are convinced of the benefits of saving. You may well be thinking to yourself—'if only I had started saving 5, 10 or 20 years ago!' No matter, the trick is to start right away. The first few years are the hardest, after which the habit of saving and the process of interest accumulation become automatic. It becomes impossible *not* to make money!

Getting the Best Interest Rate

As a taxpayer, when you invest money in a bank or building society, the interest you receive is paid net of basic rate tax. If your income is higher than the tax threshold for basic rate tax, then you will have to pay extra to the Inland Revenue when you notify them of the interest payments on your tax form. There is no legal way that you can get around this constraint in the UK, unless you are a non-taxpayer.

It is possible to open an offshore account, such as in the Channel Islands or the Isle of Man, into which interest will be paid gross. However, if you are a taxpayer and try to repatriate your profits, the Inland Revenue will take a keen interest!

There is, however, one way in which the taxpayer can get interest paid gross—by investing in a pension scheme. The government will allow you to place up to 35 per cent of your *gross* income (before tax and National Insurance deductions) in such a scheme, depending upon your age when you start investing.

You may think that investing in a pension scheme is not a particularly thrilling prospect, especially if you are young and the age of retirement seems very distant. However, stop and think about the outlook for the British economy while you are pursuing the remainder of your working life. You may have noticed that the population is ageing, and that there is a distinct shortage of young people emerging to take up the burden of producing enough to support the State welfare system.

You may ask yourself whether Britain is going to become relatively richer in the difficult years ahead, as we face increasing competition from our European partners in the EEC as well as from an ever-larger number of industrial competitors abroad. You may wonder whether any government can really address Britain's underlying economic malaise—a chronic inability to produce sufficient goods of a quality sufficient to compete in today's marketplace. You might also consider just how many competing demands there are upon the Government to provide necessary health and welfare services, and where the money is to come from to pay for these in a struggling economy.

If you are doubtful about any of these prospects, then you would, I suggest, be unwise to rely too much on State support in your old age. And when the State is handing out such tax perks to the ordinary working person, then it would be foolish not to take advantage of them.

For the debtor embarking on a repayment programme, I would also suggest that safeguarding one's pension payments is a priority, second only to absolutely essential spending on housing, food and clothing. For the person who may be reading and feeling smug because he or she is already in a pension scheme, I would suggest a careful check to ensure that full advantage is being taken of the benefits offered, so that savings close to the investment threshold are being undertaken.

Choosing a Pension Fund

It is very important that you choose a pension fund which performs well. There are hundreds to choose from, but the way to go about it is surprisingly straightforward. You must choose a fund which performs well, and you must choose a fund which will charge the least in terms of administration costs and commissions to intermediaries.

Performance figures for the various pension funds are published in the magazine *Money Management*, which is available at good newsagents. There are tables in the magazine giving performance rankings for pension funds over 5, 10 and 20 years. Choose a fund which is consistently in the top twenty in these tables.

Another tip is to choose a mutual fund. This is a company with no shareholders. Instead, profits are distributed among the policyholders of the fund, so you stand to get more of the available payouts for 'with-profits' pension and insurance policies.

As well as choosing a fund with low administration charges, it is also important that your fund does not pay commissions to intermediaries. Some funds can swallow up half of your contributions in administration costs and commissions in the first year. However, mutual funds such as London Life and Equitable Life do not pay commissions at all. This is why intermediaries are unlikely to recommend them.

Be careful if you are using an independent financial intermediary. Always ask about commission charges. In general, the funds with the lowest commissions and administration charges are the best performers, as more of your money is invested on your behalf. If your broker is unwilling to give you details of these types of funds, find another. Better still, contact the top performing companies yourself, find out about their administration charges, and make your own choice.

Friendly Societies

A little-known concession which allows you to make savings free of tax is investment in a Friendly Society savings scheme, of which there are a number. You are only allowed to pay in £9 per month; or £100 a year, but this could soon add up to a tidy sum, depending upon the performance of the fund into which you are investing.

This sort of sum is affordable for most people, and would be ideal for the person on a very low income, or for the debtor who wants painlessly to gain the savings habit. The sum realized could be used for all sorts of purposes, including perhaps a dream holiday as a future reward for getting out of debt!

TESSA Accounts

TESSA stands for Tax-Exempt Special Savings Account. This was introduced by the government in January 1991 to encourage personal savings. It allows savings of up to £9,000 for each adult over a period of five years, which may grow entirely tax free as long as it remains in the account for the whole term. You can even withdraw part of the interest during the five years without penalty, provided the remainder (which represents a notional amount of tax) is left in the account for the whole period.

TESSA accounts are subject to annual savings limits of £3,000 in the first year, and £1,800 thereafter. You can pay in lump sums or through a monthly savings scheme. The accounts are offered by banks and building societies, and it pays to shop around for the best deals, just as you would with a normal savings account.

Life Assurance

A life assurance scheme is one where in return for a monthly payment over a specified period, you are guaranteed a sizeable payout in the event of your death. Obviously, the older you are the greater your risk of death, so the premiums increase. Other risk factors such as smoking will also affect the size of the premiums paid. A variation on this type of scheme is one which assures you of an income in the event of serious disability. For people who would leave dependents such as partners and children in the event of their deaths, life assurance really should be considered essential.

There are a number of different schemes available, the most straightforward of which is term assurance, where you pay a given sum each month for life cover, but there is no lump sum due to you if you survive until the end of the term. Term assurance is the cheapest form of life cover, and can be recommended if cost is of paramount importance.

More expensive cover is available on a 'whole life' basis. This form of cover protects you for the term assured, but the policy will also pay you a lump sum if you survive until the end of the term. A 'with profits, whole life' policy will award you bonuses each year according to the performance of the company with which you are investing. Policies such as these are said to have a surrender value, and as such they can be bought and sold on the open market.

Some life-assurance schemes offer to invest part of the money on your behalf, giving you a lump sum at the end of the term in addition to life cover. These types of schemes, called endowments, are usually offered over a 10 to 20 year period, and are promoted heavily in the junk mail that comes through your letter-box courtesy of your building society or bank.

Life assurance is available tax free only if arranged in conjunction with your pension scheme. Therefore, if you are in a personal pension scheme you should ensure that you will receive tax-free basic life cover until retirement. If you want additional cover linked to endowment schemes, then by all means save in this manner, but remember to check the investment performance and commission structure of the company offering these schemes, just as you would when choosing a pension or any other kind of investment.

How to Pay Off your Mortgage in Almost Half the Time

Now, here is a fact which astonished me when I discovered it, and which I am sure will surprise you also. If you arrange to have your mortgage paid weekly instead of monthly, it will cut your repayment time by almost half, and save you many thousands of pounds.

For example suppose that you take out a loan of £50,000 at an interest rate of 15 per cent, to be repaid over a 25 year period. A conventional repayment mortgage would require a monthly repayment instalment of £560.20, which would of course repay the loan in 25 years. However, if you elected to repay £140.05 per *week*, which is one quarter of the monthly amount, then the loan would be repaid in only 16 years!

The reason for this dramatic difference is that there are 52 weeks in a year, so the annual repayment will be higher than with the monthly repayment method. It will be £7,282.60 instead of £6,722.40. The difference is magnified by the effects of reducing compound interest.

If you are paid weekly, it may be possible for you to repay a mortgage in this way. Workers paid monthly could save the difference each month and pay this into their mortgage account quarterly or annually. Either way it would make a dramatic difference to your financial health if your mortgage could be repaid quickly.

Another way of achieving the same result would be to ask your lender to recalculate your monthly payments on the basis of a shorter 16 year repayment period, and simply pay that amount each month. The difference would probably not be large enough to have a discernible affect on your standard of living.

Nonetheless, accelerated repayment of your mortgage assumes that you have a repayment mortgage; and, that you have a little bit of room to manoeuvre in repaying the small amount of extra money. If you are not in this situation, then you may well be looking for ways of *reducing* the monthly repayments. If you do this, however, it must be clear to you that it is going to add to the overall burden of repayment. For example, if you extend a simple repayment mortgage of £50,000 at 15 per cent compound interest from 25 to 30 years, your monthly repayments will be reduced from £560.20 to £546.90. However, it will have cost you an extra £28,824 to repay the mortgage by the end of the term.

Yet again, it can be seen that there are two sides of the coin to the power of compound interest. You can buy an affordable house and use the marvellous invention of mortgage credit to enjoy the house now and repay the loan over a reasonable length of time (say 15 years or so). Or you can choose to be shackled to compound interest for half a lifetime by adopting the false economy of repaying as little as you can get away with each month.

For this reason, if you consider that you are being forced by circumstances to lengthen the term of your mortgage, I would suggest that you do so in the full knowledge of what it will cost you, and with the resolution that as soon as you can you will increase the monthly repayments in order to reduce the term of the mortgage. Just stop to consider how much difference it would make to your standard of living and financial freedom if you did not have to worry about meeting mortgage repayments each month!

I will add another word of warning here. Many so-called financial advisers argue that a person should have at least a £30,000 mortgage in order to enjoy the advantage of tax relief on the interest. This argument is valid only if you can achieve a greater, low-risk rate of return from an alternative investment with the money saved. With the current high rates of interest payable on mortgages, this is very difficult to achieve. Maintaining a mortgage to allow investment elsewhere at a better rate of return is really only valid in a time of very high rates of inflation, such as during the 1970s. This strategy is unlikely to be valid in the 1990s.

Investing in Unit Trusts

Many people who are regular savers put their faith in unit trusts. Often they have replied to an advertisement in a newspaper claiming all sorts of wonderful growth records, and have invested either a lump sum or regular monthly payments into a particular trust. Until the crash of October 1987, during one of the most vigorous bull markets of this century, investors in most funds would have enjoyed substantial capital gains.

However, following the crash, the record may not have been so rosy, with a significant number of trusts having depleted the value of their holder's savings. The *average* performance of 1,000 unit trusts in 1988, the year following the crash, showed *a loss of 23.5 per cent over the twelve months*.

There was, therefore, a stampede of investors out of unit trusts during that year, with the trusts as a whole losing 10 million pounds due to net withdrawals by May 1988, down from a net inflow of more than a billion pounds in September 1987, a month before the crash.

Another less publicized feature of investment in unit trusts is the charges they incur. These are in most cases quite heavy, with an initial joining fee of around 6 per cent, and an annual management charge of 1 per cent or more. There is also a difference of 5 to 7 per cent between the prices at which you must buy units and the price at which you can sell them. Such charges can have a significant impact on your profits, or accentuate your losses.

You might also ask yourself questions about unit trust managers. If they really are professionals, why did so many suffer during the October 1987 crash? You are likely to conclude from their general lack of foresight that institutional investors are prone to behave like sheep in terms of their investment decisions. The herd instinct prevails as much among fund managers as it does among private investors.

Another possible cause for concern is the over-emphasis on the short-term performance of many funds. This partly explains the herd instinct, of course, where money managers all tend to follow the pack. No fund manager is going to be wildly different from his or her colleagues if he/she believes that it is a career risk.

However, if you accept, as I do, that there is validity in the notion of a long-term economic cycle, which is repeated throughout history, then you will also be concerned about how few fund managers share this point of view. Instead, they purport to look for 'intrinsic value' in shares which are supposedly undervalued.

If you have been following the stock-market since the crash, then you may wonder why it took many fund managers so long to realize that shares in luxury car makers such as Jaguar, had become greatly over-valued in the latter part of the 1980s. Analysts should know, of course, that glamour stocks like Jaguar, catering for conspicuous consumption, are the first to go at the end of an economic cycle.

It is no surprise that Jaguar reported half-year profits in 1989 of only

£1.4 million as compared with 1988's half-year total of £22.5 million. This compares with a peak of nearly £70 million reached in the first half of 1986, the year before the great crash.

If you respond to the advertisements for unit trusts in the press, then it is a bit like entering a lucky draw. The same may be true of asking the opinion of professional 'investment advisers', who receive commissions from unit trusts for placing business their way. These advisers would be unlikely to promote an alternative form of risk-spreading investment—the investment trust.

Investment Trusts

Investment trusts are unlike unit trusts in that they are publicly-quoted companies, which have a share price based on a stock-market valuation of their assets and performance. This price is quoted in the financial press just like any other.

The value of unit trusts, on the other hand, varies with the number of units issued, and is quoted, usually on a weekly basis, by the trust itself.

Investment trusts do not advertise much, and do not pay commissions to agents recommending them, which is why few advisers would point you in their direction. They are also generally valued below their real value, in terms of the sum of all the investments in the trust. This is of little importance to the investor unless the investment trust becomes a candidate for a take-over by another company or is converted into a unit trust, in which case, the share price is likely to leap upwards.

Investment trusts are of interest to the small investor because they have in recent years consistently outperformed unit trusts. This performance is partly accounted for by their lower level of management fees and advertising costs. Unit trust managers themselves are likely to keep part of their portfolios in shares of investment trusts.

Choosing an Investment Fund

Whether you want to invest in a unit trust, an investment trust, or a pension fund, there are certain ground rules to follow to maximize your chances of picking a winner.

There are three main steps:

- Decide the likely course of the economy.
- Pick a sector to suit the economic environment.
- Check the performance of the fund against others in its sector.

The last point would be valid even if you decided not to try to guess which way the economy was going and opted for a 'managed' fund, where the professionals make the decisions about which sectors to invest in, and what proportion of the fund should be invested in each.

There are 18 basic sectors for unit trusts, and 13 for investment trusts (listed in Appendix 4). They run the whole gamut of investment choices, from very low-risk government bonds through to high-risk trusts investing in small companies and in small overseas stock markets.

Once you have chosen the sector (or sectors) within which you want to invest, you will need to check the track record of the various funds involved—do not rely only on advertised performance figures. Obviously you will want to consider the growth rates of the funds over a five to ten year period, which would be a reflection of how well they were being managed. However, just as important as the measure of growth of a trust is the volatility of the fund—the degree to which it fluctuates within a given period.

There are three little-known measures of volatility among funds:

- *Beta value*. This tells you how risky are the shares in a trust—the higher the beta, the higher the chance of the shares fluctuating wildly.
- *Alpha value*. This tells you how well the fund manager handles the beta risk. A positive alpha value tells you that most of the time the risk has paid off. A negative alpha value tells you the opposite.
- *Standard deviation*. This tells you by how much the fund fluctuates from the average of all the other trusts in its sector. A high standard deviation means a high level of volatility.

This may all sound a bit complicated, but it is vital information for the investor. A bit of time spent thinking about your investment objectives and identifying a fund to suit them will reap you rich rewards. The alphas, betas, and standard deviation values of all UK Unit Trusts are obtainable from the *Directory of Unit Trust Management*. This is available from business libraries or can be obtained by your local library. (See Appendix 4.)

Unit trust salespeople obviously don't want you to know all this, which makes it all the more vital for you to find it out. You will also want to pay careful attention to the costs of the trusts. Otherwise, in the difficult years ahead, you may just as well keep your money in a bank or building society account.

Your Investment Objectives

Your investment objectives will depend upon two main factors—your character and your age. If you are by nature very cautious, you will most probably opt for low-risk funds. If you are a bit of a gambler, you might want to go for high-risk but potentially high-reward investments. Most people have a mixture of both characteristics, in which case it is important for you to decide *what percentage* of your funds you will keep in each type of investment.

Similarly, a person approaching retirement will be wanting to invest for a higher income, whereas a younger person will probably want to build capital. Again, a careful choice of funds or other types of investment will be necessary to ensure each particular objective.

Whatever your personal objectives and character, it is important to pay careful attention to the general state of the economy. What happens to the balance of payments, interest rates, the value of the pound in relation to other currencies and so on will have vital effects on your investment decisions. The Postscript will consider how to invest to survive a prolonged economic recession or slump.

Points to Remember

- Get into the savings habit by putting away a proportion of your income each month.
- A reputable personal pension scheme is an excellent savings vehicle, as it grows tax free.
- Join a tax-free Friendly Society or TESSA savings scheme and pick up a useful lump sum 5-10 years from now.
- Consider carefully your requirements for life assurance, and check the growth records of funds which offer investment as well as protection.
- Consider making a little extra effort to repay your mortgage early. It will make a dramatic difference to your future finances.

- Be careful when investing in unit trusts. Understand the charges made for buying and selling, and for managing the funds. Always investigate the growth record and performance variability of trusts which interest you.

- Investment trusts may offer better value for savers than unit trusts. Find out about them by contacting the trusts yourself.

- Always question intermediaries about the commissions they will receive for selling you a pension or other savings scheme. Contact the investment companies directly if you can avoid these commissions.

- Define your investment objectives just as you would any other goals. Decide what you want to achieve 5, 10 or 20 years from now, or at retirement. Plan for a prosperous future.

POSTSCRIPT

Invest for Success in the 1990s

Step 1 considered the ways in which debt has become a habit for many people, and how the explosion in personal debt during the 1980s was encouraged by the Government and by building societies, banks, and other lending institutions.

This postscript will consider the wider consequences of this lending and borrowing binge, and how you may add to the steps already taken to rid yourself of debt and provide a firm future for yourself and your family.

Before going into the details of an investment strategy for the future, it is necessary for us to go a little deeper into the background to bank lending. Then we will be able better to understand the dangers facing the world economy, and the means by which you can protect yourself.

The Background to Bank Lending

As discussed in Step 1, during the early 1980s regulations concerning institutional lending became progressively relaxed, leading to a boom in lending. This extended to mortgages given at ever higher multiples of income; liberal bank loans, some involving competitions to induce people to borrow more; and a plethora of credit card offerings.

As the credit spree developed, the banks fell over themselves to offer more and more credit, moving further and further down the economic scale and causing growing numbers of people to get into debt and ultimately to default.

There are two key reasons why the banks embarked on this policy. One is that there had been a general lack of attractive investment opportunities in new industries to soak up investors' cash. The other was that the banks had been badly burned on a previous lending spree. During the 1970s and early 1980s, banks had made extremely large, and unwise loans to the governments of developing countries. Booming prices for such commodities as oil, coffee, cocoa, cotton, copper, and tin had led the short-sighted bankers to believe that this situation would continue indefinitely and that the loans made would be invested in projects yielding a good return, and would easily be repaid.

In fact the opposite happened, and many projects turned out to be white elephants. For example, Brazil spent as much as $40 billion on nuclear power stations, none of which has yet begun to work. Or, as Susan George has pointed out in her fascinating book on Third World debt, *A Fate Worse Than Debt*, (Pelican, 1988)—the money simply found its way into the bank accounts of the corrupt rich of these developing nations, where it was used for consumption—for buying luxury goods instead of investing in industry and agriculture.

As a result of these excesses, and of the dramatic falls in commodity prices of the early 1980s, large chunks of the developing countries' debt portfolios became non-performing—in other words the debtors stopped paying interest on past loans. Currently, developing countries are estimated to owe in excess of $1 trillion to Western banks, and that debt load is rising every day.

In fact, huge amounts of debt have had to be written off by the banks, leading to losses, rather than profits, on the annual account. For example, in 1987, Barclays recorded a loss of −£248 million, while Lloyds revenue fell to −£505 million. By 1988, banks such as Midland were recording losses of over 800 million pounds!

Although problem loans to Third World countries represent the majority of most banks' bad debt, another source of bad credit is beginning to cause problems. A 1980s fashion arose for so-called 'leveraged buy-outs', where groups of managers from within a company or corporate raiders from outside bought companies by issuing thousands of high-interest bonds to investors, or by borrowing outright from banks.'Leverage' is just another name for debt. The paper issued has been nicknamed 'junk bonds', because although it pays high interest, it is also high risk.

Many of the companies purchased in this manner are in economic sectors vulnerable to a recession—notably retailing. In the UK, companies such as the retailers Lowndes Queensway and Coloroll have gone broke trying to service their borrowings. In the US the situation is if anything worse. Major banks are suffering losses as a result of having lent too much money to companies which are now unable to service their debts. One of the more notable casualties has been the property developer Donald Trump, once $3 billion in debt to the banks. This is a trend which will continue and we can expect many more tales of default from corporate debtors during the 1990s.

Seeing that losses on their existing loan portfolios were inevitable, the banks therefore cast around for other means of making big profits, and discovered the insatiable appetites of consumers in Western countries who were willing to buy now and pay later, whatever the cost! So the banks put temptation in our way, and we swallowed the bait. During the 1980s it became almost fashionable to be seen with several credit cards, and to take out one or more bank loans and hire-purchase debts—perhaps we foolishly took this as an indication of our high credit rating and consequent social status. Consumer debt in the UK mushroomed from £9.2 billion in 1980 to £36.4 billion in 1987. This represents a rise of nearly 400 per cent!

So where does this leave you and me? It is important to understand the powerful economic and social forces at work behind our own actions. Few of us are immune to prevalent social attitudes. The change in attitudes to credit and personal debt over the past decade or so was rapid, but we may have perceived it as being gradual.

Although you are certainly far from alone if you are in debt, you do need to see the situation for what it is. Imagine that debtors are a herd of cows being milked for cash by banks and finance houses! Stop giving milk and the government will be forced to reduce interest rates and financial institutions will be encouraged to start investing more money in sensible things, like factories, farms and jobs.

The explosion in the availability of credit is part of a wider economic cycle which is explained below. It is vitally important that you become familiar with this economic cycle, because it has direct effects on your financial status, and hence your whole life and well-being.

For the moment, I'm sure you will agree that the interdependence of economies in the modern world means that you cannot be blind to what happens in debtor countries such as Mexico, Argentina, and Brazil, as well as in economically-powerful ones such as Japan and the US. Equally, the travails of large corporations in the developed countries cannot be ignored. When countries and companies can't pay their debts their actions have a direct financial and emotional effect on you!

The Economic Cycle and its Direct Effects on You

The credit explosion and its unfortunate effects are a small part of a huge economic cycle in which we are all participants. It is my belief, and that of a growing number of analysts and investors, that the world economy is governed by a deep-seated cycle of events which is similar to a huge wave. It is futile trying to swim against such a powerful force, but you can learn to ride the wave. If we can all understand the basics of what happens, then we can learn to adapt to and prosper from fundamental and dramatic economic changes.

The notion of a long wave of economic activity was chiefly the theory of a Russian economist named Nikolai Kondratieff. He discovered, using economic data going back nearly two centuries, that there is apparently a regular cycle in economic activity, as measured by price rises and falls, or by the volume of industrial production.

To cut a long story short, he identified a long upswing lasting 25 to 30 years, and a long downswing of similar length. Each part of the cycle is marked by booms and recessions, except that during the upswing the booms are strong and long and the recessions weak and short. During the downswing, the opposite happens: the recessions are deep and severe, the booms shallow and short.

I first heard of Kondratieff while studying economics at university. At the time, his work was considered an interesting but insufficiently proven footnote to the main body of economic theory, whether capitalist or Marxist. Under Stalin's regime Kondratieff was imprisoned (where he eventually died) for failing to preach the 'correct' Marxist gospel, which said that booms and slumps are strictly capitalist phenomena. Kondratieff argued, on the contrary, that economic gyrations are international. He also managed to predict correctly that the world would go into a slump in the 1930s.

During the 1980s my interest in Kondratieff's work was rekindled. This happened because my work at the time alerted me the escalation of unpayable national debt in the Third World, while events in the UK were similarly disturbing. The early 1980s saw Britain facing the worst recession of modern times, when daily news bulletins told of factory closures, when the unemployment rate rose from one million to more than three million, and when 20 per cent of British industrial capacity disappeared.

These problems persisted for much of the decade, and not just in Britain but in the whole of Europe and the US as well. Meanwhile, Third

World countries, particularly in Latin America and Africa were suffering from a downright depression, with the prices of their export commodities falling to their lowest levels in 50 years. The only bright star on the horizon was the Far East, where the 'Newly-Industrialized Countries' (NICS) such as Taiwan and South Korea were taking off, along with Asia's only economically advanced country, Japan.

The continued prosperity of certain Asian countries marks a fundamental shift in world economic activity, from West to East. This does not mean that the Asian economies are immune to global recessionary forces, but their vigour and enthusiasm *does* ensure that they can adapt rapidly to changing conditions. Moreover, the burgeoning Chinese and Japanese markets represent massive sources of future growth as their populations grow bigger and richer, demanding more and more goods and services.

Unfortunately, the ability of North America and Europe to provide goods and services in sufficient quantity and of sufficient quality to preserve their economic supremacy is increasingly in doubt. Some Japanese industrialists have contemptuously referred to 'America as our farm, and Europe as our boutique', meaning that they expect to get a good chunk of the mass markets for everyday manufactured goods.

Nevertheless, the US is still the engine of world economic growth, accounting for around 13 per cent of world trade. But it is losing confidence in its ability to sell its goods in the face of cut-throat competition. As we near the end of Kondratieff's projected cycle, old industries have matured, and there are fewer and fewer opportunities for profitable investment in industry. Instead, money has been poured into retailing, property, and financial assets. There is a chronic surfeit of most categories of manufactured goods, with the exception of some products based on new technologies, such as advanced microchips—although don't forget that even the relatively new computer market is already saturated.

The frenzied competition among nations for market share in the sale of goods and services is leading to calls for protectionism. The US, for example, is very uneasy about the decreasing access for its goods within the European Common Market (especially in agriculture), and is downright angry about the flood of cheap high technology Far Eastern exports. Often, the US has accused Japan or other Far Eastern countries of dumping goods on the market at cheap prices to gain market share. However, it is just as often the case that American goods are plainly uncompetitive.

The US paranoia manifested itself in a trade bill, passed in 1988, which enables it to introduce retaliatory measures in response to this 'dumping'. The bill can be used to protect any US market. At the time of writing, Japan, Korea, Taiwan and the EEC countries (among others) have already been put on the hit list for probable retaliation by the US for 'unfair' trading practices.

Depressionary Aspects of the Long Wave

The depression of the 1930s was not really caused by the stock market crash of 1929—this was but a symptom of the underlying malaise. It was brought about principally by the previous accumulation of debt and the introduction of a protectionist trade law—known as the Smoot-Hawley bill—which was signed in 1930 by President Hoover. The bill allowed for protection of US industry in the face of foreign competition, and was rapidly followed by similar retaliatory laws in other countries. World trade shrank dramatically, and the Great Depression resulted.

There is a distinct danger that protectionism could re-emerge in the 1990s. In the short run, protectionism may give the illusion of protecting jobs, but it will rapidly lead to a fall in world trade as more and more nations introduce tariffs on imports. This destroys many more jobs dependent on world trade than it protects.

It is easy then to see why so much credit has been made available, and why so many of us have gone heavily into debt. Investors have not tended to put money into manufacturing or raw materials production, because in a time of saturated markets the returns on these activities have not been very attractive. Instead funds have gone into shops, services, shares and property—the very industries which have benefited most from the credit explosion.

Unfortunately, the underlying malaise has grown. During the mid-1980s, when the price of my little flat began to shoot up, making my paper wealth grow from negative figures to quite a respectable sum in the space of a couple of years, I was at first at a loss to understand the reason. I knew that there was still high unemployment, industrial decline, and debt, yet the Government and the economic pundits were speaking of a revival.

In fact, what we were witnessing was the type of short, shallow boom characteristic of the downside part of the Kondratieff cycle. This was to a great extent fuelled by borrowing, especially in the US. 'Reaganomics' relied heavily on borrowing from foreigners to pay for a consumer boom which turned a net surplus of $200 billion worth of income from US assets overseas into a net debt of one trillion dollars ($1,000,000,000,000!) debt in seven short years (1982 through 1988). The rest of the developed world is supposed to have benefited from this expansion, as the US bought up imports, but the debts still have to be paid.

If we examine the Kondratieff wave as a whole, we can see that the last cycle bottomed in the mid 1930s, and the long boom took us right up to the mid 1970s. The sharp recession of 1972 to 74 saw share prices in the UK fall by 85 per cent, representing the first severe recession since the war. Some observers of the time saw this as the end of modern capitalism.

The subsequent recovery saw raging inflation, a characteristic of the peak of the Kondratieff cycle, followed by another recession, the nasty experience of 1979-82. Industrial production in some sectors halved at this time.

The final financial insanity of the 1980s followed, which we have now seen come to an end. The City, property, and retailing became the new glamour industries while a rather sickening display of rampant materialism affected the nation. Madonna sang about being a 'Material Girl', and young men in their mid-twenties earned telephone number salaries. People in more ordinary jobs could be forgiven for feeling rather hard done by as advertisements emblazoned the values of the 1980s 'yuppy' across the nation.

The Depression of the 1990s

The stock-market crash of October 1987, which was almost twice as bad (in terms of the percentage decline of the stock indices in London and New York) as that of 1929, marked the end of what is almost certainly the last boom of the downwave.

The 1990s, according to this theory, should see value systems reversed, and the old glamour industries cut down to size. The City has been the first to go, followed by property, and then retailing. The effects on other service industries and manufacturing will be felt in due course.

Evidence is growing of a slump in business in the 1990s in many industries. For example, the demand for foreign holidays has dropped dramatically; industrial designers face savage cutbacks; advertising firms have felt the pinch; furniture manufacturers are cutting back on investment and are shedding jobs; clothing retailers are closing down branches; and estate agents are going bust.

If you work in one of these sectors, or another which is equally vulnerable, you may already be thinking of changing your job, or about getting a great deal more competitive in order to keep it! Believe it or not, there is still room for lots of optimism. The Chinese character for danger can also be read to mean opportunity. If you are brave, willing to adapt, and do not delude yourself by believing the platitudes of politicians and others with vested interests, who always tell us that everything is under control and that an upturn is just around the corner, then there are still lots of opportunities. But you must learn to look after yourself.

Take property as an example: In 1990, we were all earnestly assured that property values could only go up, and that at worst they would plateau out before resuming an upward trend. Strangely enough, by mid-year house prices had fallen by up to 25 per cent in parts of southern England, where the boom first started. The same pundits who told us that prices would never fall comfortingly told us that this is would only be a 'correction' and that prices would inevitably shoot up again.

If Kondratieff is right, and we are nearing the end of the long-term economic cycle, then this simply cannot be the case. The opposite is more likely to be true—housing has been the subject of a popular mania, a speculative boom which has now burst, and prices must continue to fall. This should lead all of us to review what housing means to us—an investment or a place to live?

I am not suggesting that the world is a simple place, or that the workings of the global economy are straightforward and can be predicted to a definite timetable. Bob Beckman author of *The Downwave: Surviving the Second Great Depression* (EP Dutton, 1986) made this mistake in the early 1980s when he foresaw the end of the property and stock market booms 5 to 6 years too early. Yet he was correct in his general forecast. There is a logic in the sequence of events currently being played out.

So far we have had the stock-market crash, followed by the effects on property; followed by the retail crunch. It is not just caused by high interest rates—they are merely a symptom of the underlying crisis of the British and international economies.

My anticipation for the rest of the 1990s is a rise in unemployment, a continuing bear market (earmarked by falling prices) in shares and property, and a rising tide of protectionism—whereby markets become more and more fortified against outside penetration. In other words, another recession. If the protectionist beast is allowed out of its cage, then we shall have a full-blooded depression, with the world splitting up into antagonistic trading blocks.

In the past, depressions have often been followed by wars—and if this tendency continues, we could be looking at one, fought against one or several Far Eastern countries (Europe's major economic competitors) early in the next century. China, in particular, will be feeling under threat due to the disintegration of the Soviet empire and the gradual realignment of its republics and satellite countries with the West.

This may sound over-dramatic. I certainly do not want this chain of events to happen. But I cannot help believing that the evidence of 200 years of economic history does point to a strong economic cycle, which has a direct bearing on social and political behaviour.

The sooner we all dump unsustainable consumer debt the better, then the world can then work out the cycle, avoid protectionism and war, and get on with the task of investing in new industries, jobs and peace. It certainly wouldn't hurt for us all to put our personal finances in order once again!

Surviving the Economic Slump of the 1990s

If you are even half-convinced that we are in danger of a recession—or worse, a depression—in the 1990s, then you will be anxious to take action to avoid its effects. There are two basic principles here which I suggest you adopt. The first is to *keep it simple*, and the second is to *minimize risk*. This latter principle is particularly important if you are a bit of a risk-taker by nature, for I would suggest to you that now is the time to develop reserves of caution.

The future is full of uncertainty. The Kondratieff devotee has only a rough guide to follow, and while understanding the long-term wave of economic behaviour, can run into a lot of trouble through failing to take account of short-term variations in economic activity. I see it as a voyage through uncharted seas, where one is constantly trying to avoid mines and other barely-seen obstructions.

We do not know how bad the bad times will be, or for how long they will last. Some analysts fear that because the stock-market crash was so severe (twice as bad as 1929's), that the ensuing depression will be much worse than that of the 1930s. Others hope for a so-called 'soft landing'.

Nobody can predict with any real accuracy whether the necessary purging of debt from the world economic system will be hyper-inflationary (with rapidly rising prices) or deflationary (with falling prices). Several Latin American debtor countries, for example, have chosen to print reams of banknotes in an effort to deal with their economic woes, with devastating effects through hyper-inflation (running at thousands of per cent a year) on the living standards of their peoples.

The Thatcher Government, when it was first elected, said that the rate of increase in the money supply would be kept under rigid control. During the early 1980s, this strategy was followed, worsening the effects of the severe recession which demolished 20 per cent of Britain's industrial capacity. Just when British industry needed cheap credit to get it through the bad times, it faced very expensive credit which it could ill-afford.

In the latter half of the 1980s, the Government abandoned its position and allowed the supply of money to increase by around 20 per cent a year, fuelled in part by an explosion in the availability of credit. This is inflationary, and the direct reversal of the previously cherished monetarist policy.

My own view is that inflation in this country will gradually fall, although remaining much higher than among our competitors. I also believe that the UK will continue to be the weakest of the richer economies, second only to Australia. The US may not suffer as much as the European countries, and, if so, will gradually reduce its trade deficit. This will happen because the US economy is so large and entrepreneurial, with self-sufficiency in many commodities, products and services that will not be too badly hit by a decline in trade. There is likely to be over the long-term a strengthening US dollar, the pound falling relative to it.

Investment strategy under these conditions would imply the priorities discussed below:

Build Cash Reserves

Remember that *cash is king* during a depression. People with cash can pick up amazing bargains. This is true of almost any goods you can think of. Large electrical appliances, cars, stereos, TVs, videos, fridges, cookers, and all the other gadgets and labour saving devices of modern life will get cheaper and cheaper as retailers fight to move stocks. Clothing sales will also become a permanent spectacle on the high street as retailers struggle for turnover.

In the UK housing market, staggering bargains will become possible for cash buyers. Since October 1987 houses in the US are routinely purchased for as little as a third of their pre-crash value. You can have a four-bedroomed house built for you in Houston, including a swimming pool and every gadget you care to think of, for around £40,000. This fact may indicate just how far the UK housing market has got to fall before its prices become reasonable again.

If you put cash into a building society or bank account, you will get a reasonably high interest rate, about two points above the rate of inflation. Your cash will be secure, and you can enjoy the luxury of waiting and saving. The longer you wait, the more money you will save when you come to buy goods which few others can afford. If you are currently thinking of making a large purchase—be patient!

A word of warning about cash savings is in order here. Bank and building society deposits in the UK are only protected up to a level of £20,000. The protection given is 70 per cent of deposits below this level for banks; and 80 per cent for building societies. Avoid deposits in excess of £20,000 in any one account; and choose the biggest banks and building societies. The smaller institutions could well go under during a depression.

In particular, the smaller banks and building societies offering the highest interest rates are the ones making the highest-risk loans to service the interest rates paid to depositors. Avoid them like the plague—remember that as many as a third of the building societies (savings and loan companies) in the US had gone bankrupt by 1990.

Investment in Government Bonds

A near alternative to cash, and also very safe, is investment in Government bonds, also known as gilt-edged securities, or *gilts*. These represent money borrowed by the Government to finance its 'Public Sector Borrowing Requirement' (PSBR), which represents the difference between what the Government receives in taxes and what it has to pay out to run essential services. In recent times, we have had the opposite—a 'Public Sector Debt Repayment' (PSDR), whereby the Government has repurchased gilts.

The gilts market is huge—about 50 per cent bigger than the stock market. It is also highly liquid, meaning that it is easy to buy and sell gilts. You can do so either through a stockbroker or through the Post Office—National Savings runs a register of Government stock. It is cheaper but slower to buy and sell through National Savings rather than a stockbroker.

Government bonds are issued at a fixed rate of interest, reflecting contemporary economic conditions. For example, bonds issued half a century ago carry an extremely low rate of interest of 2 or 3 per cent; whereas bonds issued during the inflationary 1970s may carry interest rates of 16 or 17 per cent. Therefore, in relation to current interest rates, low-interest bonds trade at less than their face value, and high-interest bonds at more than their face value. However, when the bonds are redeemed at the end of their life, they are repaid at face value. You might pay only £90 for a bond paying 8 per cent per annum interest with a face value of £100 in 1991. However, when you redeem it in 1996, it will be worth £100. Obviously, if interest rates go up, the value of your bond will fall. If interest rates fall, the value of your bond will rise.

The short-to-medium term outlook for interest rates is difficult. It really depends upon the Government's willingness to defend the pound by keeping interest rates high as opposed to its willingness to ease recessionary pressure by reducing them. On the basis of past performance, we might expect the government to put the defence of the pound first, as a rule.

However, at some point, as interest rates begin to fall worldwide and Governments make desperate attempts to stimulate sluggish economies, it will be worth investing in Government bonds. In the meantime, you might like to consider buying 'short dated' bonds, whose yield can be very high, nearly 12 per cent annually at the time of writing. Short-dated bonds are a lot safer than money in the bank.

Longer-dated bonds are more speculative, and will do well if interest rates fall firmly. However, they are more volatile, with all the risks that entails. At least with a short-dated bond you know you will get your money back within five years or less, and they pay a high rate of interest. Also, if interest rates rise, their tradable value will not fall by as much as longer-dated bonds.

A bull market in bonds will appear at some point, while the share market falls to levels most people would previously have believed to be impossible. So watch out for it, and benefit from your prudence. In the meantime, keep accumulating cash.

Other Types of Bonds

Government bonds are good: they are very secure, very liquid, and pay a good rate of interest. You should remember, however, that the interest is taxed. (although capital gains brought about by astute investment in government bonds are not yet taxed).

Other types of bonds should be treated with extreme caution. These include bonds issued by debtor nations, such as Mexico and Brazil, by debtor local authorities; and by highly indebted companies.

These last are known as 'junk bonds', because although they pay high rates of interest, they are high-risk. As we have seen, many are the result of so-called 'leveraged buy-outs', when the management of a company or a group of outsiders borrow huge sums of money in order to buy the company.

There was a mania for these kinds of deals during the 1980s, but they then began to turn sour. In the UK, certain large retailers saw their share prices slump as a result of inability to service debts; while the stock-market in the US was rocked by rumours of the incipient failure of major banks which have funded too many leveraged buy-outs.

The message to the investor who is thinking of buying any of the debt of such suspect borrowers is—don't, no matter how attractive the interest rate. It simply isn't worth the risk.

The bonds of blue-chip companies, rated 'triple A' debtors, the safest of the safe, are a different matter. They can for the most part be purchased safely, especially in the aftermath of an economic scare, when their prices may be temporarily depressed.

Investment in Gold

Gold is traditionally a hedge against inflation, rather than depression, although some people like to keep all or part of their assets in gold during chaotic times. In 1990 the price of gold was quite low, down from the heady days of the early 1980s when it reached over $800 an ounce, to its 1990 level of around $350 to $400.

The price of gold may continue to drift downwards as deflationary forces grip the world economy. It is unlikely to rise spectacularly, unless there is a financial panic brought on by the mass repudiation of sovereign debt, or the failure of sufficient numbers of corporate issuers of junk bonds. Any such jump in price would probably be short-lived.

Dealing in gold, then, is rather speculative. However, in the event that the depression takes a hyper-inflationary course, at some point gold may well be resurrected as a reserve 'currency' for the world, replacing the once-mighty dollar. If this happens, its value will shoot up. Holders of gold or gold shares may well benefit.

If gold is effectively nationalized, as it was in the 1930s, it would become illegal for private investors to hold it, and would be purchased at an artificially low price. In such circumstances, gold *shares* would be worth considering, as it is unlikely these would be nationalized.

Investment in Foreign Currencies

You will remember that the pound is likely to weaken over the 1990s, perhaps spectacularly as foreign investors take fright at Britain's persistently high inflation, resurrected labour disputes, and constant tendency to import a great deal more than it exports.

Membership in the European Exchange Rate Mechanism implies greater stability for the pound. However, the UK may be required to maintain high-interest rates as the price of this stability.

Exchange rate uncertainties make it worthwhile for the saver to consider keeping part of his or her cash in a reliable foreign currency. The interest rate paid would be less than that paid in sterling, but this would quite probably be more than compensated for by the increase in the foreign currency's value when converted into sterling. The deutschmark and the dollar are good bets, and it is straightforward to open an account in either. Just ask one of the 'big four' banks for details (Barclays, Lloyds, NatWest, and Midland).

Investment in Unit or Investment Trusts

By all means think about entrusting some of your money to unit or investment trusts that are investing in sectors likely to do well in the 1990s, such as government bonds both in the UK and overseas, or companies likely to do well in the changing economic environment (such as some of the new technology trusts, for example). However, do please check out the validity of the claims made by the salespeople, many of whom may know very little and care even less about trust appraisal. Examine the growth records by all means, but remember also to consider the risk and volatility of the funds. The tools with which you can appraise trust performance are outlined in Step 10.

Investment in Shares

Most unit trusts, managed pension funds and the like are heavily invested in shares, or *equities* as they are otherwise known. Because share price performance over the past three decades has been so extraordinarily good, many people believe that the majority of their investments should continue to be in shares.

However, the tremendous growth in share values has corresponded to the upswing in the long economic cycle as identified by Kondratieff. Also, concealed within this long upswing are periods of sharp reversal. In the stock-market crash of 1987, shares lost some 30 per cent of their value before recovering. A few people may also recall the UK stock-market crash of 1972 to 1975, when the stock market index lost 85 per cent of its value! Shares can give you a roller coaster ride—they are quite risky investments.

In times of great uncertainty, it is best to steer clear of the stock market. At the very least share prices, even of the largest blue-chip companies, are likely to be highly volatile. Overall, the stock exchange indices, such as the Dow Jones index in New York, and the FTSE 100 in London, have shown share prices moving sideways, not upwards, since the great crash of 1987. The Nikkei average in Tokyo has also shown some pretty savage losses.

The long wave economic cycle suggests that shares plunge in value internationally as global recession causes world debt to be eliminated through global recession. The length of time over which this takes place remains uncertain—it may take over a decade to be completed, or it may only take a few years.

In my opinion, it is best to steer clear of the stock-market during the early to mid-1990s, at least until the process of global debt elimination has been completed. Keep your money in cash or Government bonds, and pick up share bargains at the bottom of the cycle.

Investing in Yourself

Probably the most important investment you can make is in your own skills and motivation. You will need to take a long hard look at your occupation and decide whether or not it is likely to survive the kind of economic upheaval likely in a world purging itself of debt. If you decide that your job may be in danger, then the time has come to consider taking steps to open up other avenues of employment.

New skills can be learned part-time at your local technical college. You may be fortunate enough to obtain day release from work to attend college, otherwise you will need to go to evening classes. Perhaps you have always longed to follow a particular career but have neglected to do anything about it for fear of failure, or of what your friends may think, or any of other the countless reasons one might invent as excuses. Now is the time to take action to put yourself on a new road.

If you are casting around for occupational inspiration, a few tips might help. Occupations which help to save people money, or which serve basic needs, will do well in a depression. Stay away from the luxury trades and from the glamour service industries of the 1980s, such as retailing, finance, advertising and recruitment—unless you are really confident of your abilities. Some individuals and firms will do well in every sector during hard times, but you can minimize your chances of financial pain by picking a healthy economic sector.

Life for the small businessperson is likely to be hard over the next few years, unless overheads can be cut to the bone. Many people will consider themselves lucky to have a job in a large corporation or in the Civil Service. Certainly employees will become less cavalier in their attitude to changing jobs. Many people will be glad of a safe if relatively poorly-paid job. Nevertheless, you should endeavour to put yourself in a position where you can enjoy your occupation.

If you have been thinking of undertaking part-time work, the sooner you start the better. The extra money can be put to work immediately to reduce debt, or to save for bargains in the future. Part-time work which will be easiest to get will be in sales. If you can take the time to learn how to sell, and pick products which will help people save money or improve their health, then you could make a good part-time income. Remember that with a positive mental attitude you can become a great salesperson, and be rewarded in direct proportion to your efforts, unlike many jobs where you earn much the same as your colleagues, whether you perform well or poorly.

Alternatively, you may be able to identify products or services that you can make or provide yourself from home, on a part-time basis. By avoiding the middle-men you will be able to keep costs down, and therefore prices will also be low. Give people a bargain and they will flock to buy. The popularity of open-air markets and car boot sales is proof positive of the healthy demand for bargain goods. This demand can only increase during hard times. Don't be afraid to be enterprising, and to take advantage of the mood of the times.

Conclusion

Investors in the 1990s have to be extremely cunning in order to protect their wealth. The days of picking shares virtually at random, and seeing them rise remorselessly, are well and truly over. The 1980s bull market represented the last-but-one gasp of the economic cycle. Massive debt was accumulated, and must now be purged from the system. The days of the borrower are numbered, while the saver, who was previously savaged by inflation, is doing well.

I cannot stress too strongly the need for people to get out of debt and build cash reserves as an absolute priority. More sophisticated investment strategies are all very well, but you must get the basics sorted out first.

During the financially manic 1980s, many of us built up debt burdens on a scale simply unthinkable in our parents' or grandparents' generation. It seemed for a while that prosperity would go on and on. However, the whole shallow boom was fuelled by borrowing, whether by individuals, companies or whole countries. The time has come to pay the piper, and if the debt cannot be paid, the tune will be a desolate one.

It is also important to realize that very few influential people in positions of power will have the vision or the bravery to admit just how bad the situation really is and will be. No government politician would risk his or her career by telling people what is really going on. When you hear anyone talking on the TV or radio about the economy, you can bet he or she is an 'expert' with a vested interest: an estate agent spouting forth about houses; or a stockbroker going on about economic prospects. Such people are not neutral, they will always want to minimize the dangers we face in order to keep earning their commissions. They will always tell us that good times are just around the corner.

Those of us out in the real world, making, selling and buying things, trying to pay the bills and experiencing the real economy, already know of real difficulties. Nevertheless, it is not too late to face problems and deal with them. You can take action now to protect yourself and your family. Deal with your debt; start saving; use your subconscious mind to identify opportunities to allow you to profit even in difficult times.

The tools you need to make a start and follow it through are in this book. You have nothing to worry about. With a positive mental attitude you can and will be successful. So don't waste any more time—get out of debt and prosper!

Appendices

Appendix 1
Sources of Information and Advice

The Association of Bankrupts, 4 Johnson Close, Abraham Heights, Lancaster, LA1 5EU. Tel: 0254 64305. Advice, support and information for actual or potential bankrupts.

The Building Societies Association, 3 Savile Row, London W1X 1AF. Tel: 071 437 0655. Publishes a free leaflet for borrowers on coping with arrears. The BSA has also developed guidelines for dealing with arrears. Get hold of a copy to use as ammunition when negotiating with your lender.

Building Society Helplines. Some building societies have telephone helplines, for example the Leeds Permanent and Bradford and Bingley. You might check with your lender to see if they offer a similar service.

Foster and Cranfield, 20 Britton Street, London EC1M 5NQ. Tel: 071 608 1941. Auctioneers of endowment policies, with auctions being held monthly.

Gas Consumers Council, Abford House, 15 Wilton Road, London SW1V 1LT. Tel: 071 608 1941. Offers free, independent advice to people having trouble paying their bills, and can liaise with creditors on their behalf through consumer advisors.

Gingerbread, 35 Wellington Street, London WC2E 7BN. Tel: 071 240 0953. An organization offering a national support network of self-help groups for one-parent families.

The National Association of Citizen's Advice Bureaux, 115-123 Pentonville Road, London N1 9LZ. Tel: 071 823 2181. The nearest branch will also be listed in your phone book. The CAB will be able to give you help and may refer you to a Money Advice Centre to help you construct a spending plan and to negotiate with creditors.

The National Consumer Council, 18 Queen Anne's Gate, London SW1 9AA. Tel: 071 222 9501.

National Debtline: 021 359 8501. Based in Birmingham, this free advice centre will send you information on reorganizing your finances as well as offering advice over the phone.

Office of Electricity Regulation, Hagley House, Hagley Road, Birmingham B16 8QG. Tel: 021 456 2100. Offers information and advice for electricity consumers, and can negotiate on behalf of those in financial difficulty. Call the head office for information on your nearest regional office.

Office of Fair Trading, Chancery House, 53 Chancery Lane, London WC2A 1SP. Tel: 071 242 2858. This Government department publishes two helpful booklets: 'Creditwise, Your Guide to Trouble-Free Credit' and 'Debt, a Survival Guide'. Both are available free.

Policy Network, 68 Chandos Place, London WC2N 4HG. Tel: 071 929 2971. A broking service which puts potential buyers of with-profits endowment policies in touch with sellers.

Relate (formerly the National Marriage Guidance Council), Herbert Gray College, Little Church Street, Rugby CV21 3AP. Tel: 0788 73241. Call for information and help if your relationship with your partner is under too much strain.

Samaritans, listed in your telephone directory, for a sympathetic ear, help and advice when the going gets tough.

Shelter, 157 Waterloo Road, London SE1. Tel: 071 633 9377. A national charity which can give advice if you are threatened with the loss of your home.

If you have a question or problem concerning credit you can also telephone your local **Trading Standards Office**; the address will be in your phone book.

Appendix 2   **Recommended reading**

There are quite a number of books available which are relevant to the topics we have discussed. Here are a few key titles which are recommended as additional support for the reader who is truly determined to get out of debt and prosper.

Personal Development

Hill, Napoleon. *Think and Grow Rich*, Los Angeles: Wilshire Book Company, 1970.

Holland, Ron. *Talk and Grow Rich*, Wellingborough: Thorsons, 1981.

Patent, Arnold. *You Can Have It All: The Art of Winning the Money Game and Living a Life of Joy*, Forest Row, Sussex: New Age, 1984.

Schwartz, David. *The Magic of Thinking Big*, Wellingborough: Thorsons, 1984.

Eliminating Debt and Increasing Income

Delderfield, Paul. *Successful Borrowing and Coping with Debt*, London: Daily Telegraph Publications, 1987.

Denny, Richard. *Selling to Win*, London: Kogan Page, 1988.

Lines, Tony. *The Penguin Guide to Supplementary Benefits*, Harmondsworth: Penguin Books, 1987.

Lubbock, Bill and Stokes, Richard. *How to Get a Job*, London: Hamlyn, 1989.

Tait, Nikki. *The Investors Chronicle Beginner's Guide to the Stockmarket*, Harmondsworth: Penguin Books, 1987.

The Debt Crisis and Investment in the 1990s

Batra, Ravi. *The Great Depression of 1990*, New York: Bantam Books, 1988.

Beckman, Robert. *The Downwave: Surviving the Second Great Depression*, New York: EP Dutton, 1986.

Congdon, Tim. *The Debt Threat*, Oxford: Basil Blackwell, 1988.

Davidson, J.D. and Rees-Mogg, W. *Blood in the Streets: Investment Profits in a World Gone Mad*, London: Sidgwick and Jackson, 1988.

George, Susan. *A Fate Worse than Debt*, Harmondsworth: Pelican, 1988.

Wood, Christopher. *Boom and Bust: The Rise and Fall of the World's Financial Markets*, London: Sidgwick and Jackson, 1988.

Appendix 3   Formula for Calculating Compound Interest

The formula for calculating compound interest on a debt or investment is not very difficult, although you will need to use a calculator. It is as shown in Table 15:

$$A = P \times \left(1 + \frac{R}{100}\right)^t$$

Where A = the final amount of the debt/investment

P = the principal sum borrowed/invested

R = the rate of interest

t = the time period over which it is borrowed/invested

For example, let us say that you borrow £1,000 for five years at an interest rate of 20% per annum. At the end of the period you will owe:

$$A = £1,000 \times \left(1 + \frac{20}{100}\right)^5$$

$$A = £1,000 \times (1 + 0.2)^5$$

$(1 + 0.2^5)$ is 1.2 multiplied by itself five times, or 2.488

$$A = £1,000 \times 2.488$$

$$A = £2,488$$

After borrowing £1,000 for five years at an interest rate of 20 per cent per annum, you will owe the lender £2,488.

Appendix 4 **Unit and Investment Trust Sectors**

The potential investor in Unit Trusts has a basic choice to make—whether to aim for capital growth or for income. Once that decision has been made, he or she must choose between the geographical or economic sector, and then check the record of the funds listed in the sector(s) chosen.

Unit Trust Sectors

There are 18 Unit trust sectors, which are as follows:
1. UK General—75 per cent or more invested in the UK, aiming for both income and capital growth.
2. UK Growth—capital growth is the priority here, with higher risk but a potentially higher reward.
3. UK Equity Income—aiming for steady yield through investment primarily in UK companies.
4. UK Mixed Income—going for yield but spreading risk through investment in preference and fixed-interest stocks as well as ordinary shares.
5. Gilt and Fixed Interest Growth—low risk with growth objectives.
6. Gilt and Fixed Interest Income—as above, but aiming for steady income.
7. Investment Trusts—growth-oriented trusts primarily buying into Investment Trusts.
8. Financial and Property—generally growth-oriented.
9. International Growth—worldwide investment, particularly in the USA and Japan.
10. International income—as above, but with more of an emphasis on bonds and high yielding stocks.
11. North America Growth—80 per cent or more invested in the USA and Canada.
12. European Growth—80 per cent or more invested in European markets, including trusts specializing in single countries such as Germany.
13. Australian Growth—investing primarily in Australian companies, particularly in gold and minerals sectors.
14. Japanese Growth—a wide spectrum of growth-oriented investment in Japanese companies.
15. Far Eastern Growth—aiming for rapid appreciation in the Pacific and East Asian countries.
16. Commodity and Energy—worldwide investment in these sectors, primarily for growth.

17. Managed Trusts—investing in other unit trusts run by the same company.
18. Exempt Trusts—specialising in charitable bodies and pension funds.

The performance records of Unit Trusts can be derived from the *Directory of Unit Trust Management*, London: Stock Exchange Press, International Publishers Ltd. See also the *Unit Trust Yearbook*, London: Financial Times Business Information.

Investment Trust Sectors

There are 13 sectors identified for Investment Trusts. They are similar in composition to those identified for Unit Trusts. The sectors are as follows:

1. Capital and Income Growth: General
2. Capital and Income Growth: UK
3. Capital Growth: General
4. Capital Growth: International
5. Capital Growth: North America
6. Capital Growth: Far East
7. Capital Growth: Japan
8. Capital Growth: Commodity and Energy
9. Capital Growth: Technology
10. Income Growth
11. Smaller Companies
12. Special Features
13. Split Capital Trusts

For further information, contact: *The Association of Investment Trust Companies*, Parkhouse, 16 Finsbury Circus, London EC2M MJJ. Tel: 071 588 5347.

Index